£1-00

C000199653

STUDIES IN THE UK
Mrs Thatcher's
economics

Mrs Thatcher's economics

David Smith
Economics Correspondent of *The Times*

HEINEMANN
EDUCATIONAL

For my father

Heinemann Educational,
a division of Heinemann Educational Books Ltd,
Halley Court, Jordan Hill, Oxford OX2 8EJ

OXFORD LONDON EDINBURGH
MELBOURNE SYDNEY AUCKLAND
SINGAPORE MADRID IBADAN
NAIROBI GABORONE HARARE
KINGSTON PORTSMOUTH NH

First published 1988
Reprinted 1989

British Library Cataloguing in Publication Data
Smith, David
   Mrs. Thatcher's economics. — (Studies in
   the UK economy).
   1. Great Britain. Economic policies
   I. Title II. Series
   330.941 '0858

ISBN 0 435 33002 0

Typeset and illustrated by Gecko Limited, Bicester, Oxon

Printed and bound in Great Britain by Biddles Ltd, King's Lynn and Guildford

Acknowledgements

Grateful thanks are due to my wife Jane for her forbearance. Mention must
also be made of my sons Richard and Thomas, in spite of whom this was
written, and my daughter Emily, who was too young to know what was going
on. Thanks too to Bryan Hurl of Harrow School, who acted as a very capable
midwife on the project.

Thanks are also due to the following for permission to reproduce copyright
material: The Controller of Her Majesty's Stationery Office for the tables on
pp.10, 52, 53, 54, 58, 69, 71 and for the graphs on pp.21 and 30; Martin
Robertson for the extracts on pp.26 and 32; *Times Newspapers Limited* for
the articles on pp.18–19, 37–8, 39–40, 59–60, 77–8, 79–80.

Preface

Mrs Thatcher's economic policies frequently cause heated debate and disagreement but whatever one's normative views, her economics cannot be ignored. To challenge them necessitates being informed. To support them requires judgement as to their successes and failures.

As a professional communicator David Smith has been well placed to study and explain these policies during the '80s at a level which is appropriate for this series for schools and colleges. He charts the rise and fall of monetarism, the pursuit of the enterprise culture, people's capitalism, privatization and trade union reform. Particularly apt are his own articles from *The Times* reproduced as data response questions. Here is both applied economics vibrant with its relevance, and economic theory combined with current living economics in the making.

Bryan Hurl
Series Editor

Contents

Chapter One
An introduction to a changing economy

The purposes of this book are to explain the principles underlying Mrs Thatcher's economics, to examine the way in which the different elements of policy are carried out, and to assess some of the long-term and short-term effects.

The British economy has undergone enormous change since the election of Mrs Margaret Thatcher as Prime Minister on 3 May 1979. Some see that change as entirely for the good, with the elimination of inflation as a signficant danger, the emergence of new attitudes in business and industry which have brought rapid growth in productivity and a new mood of realism in industrial relations – in marked contrast with the spirit of self-destruction of the 1960s and 70s.

Critics of Mrs Thatcher and her government are, however, unwilling to accept the claimed benefits of the economic policies pursued since 1979. They are quick to cite the economic damage that those policies have incurred. Thus, the critics say, low inflation is a worldwide phenomenon in which Britain has been a lucky participant. High growth in productivity, or output per worker, is a temporary phenomenon brought about by the shedding of labour by industry on a massive scale; and high unemployment is itself the result of mistakenly harsh monetary and fiscal policies. Meanwhile, the critics say, the economy has been kept afloat through the good fortune of possessing one non-renewable asset – North Sea oil – and by the steady disposal of a limited stock of assets – state industries – by privatization.

Our task here is not primarily to take sides in this debate. The essential point is that no observer of the economic scene in Britain would dispute that the landscape has changed, in some cases beyond recognition. The period since 1979 has clearly been a very important one for economic policy.

Four principles
Sir Geoffrey Howe, the first Chancellor of the Exchequer under Mrs Thatcher, set the scene for subsequent policy in his Budget speech on 12 June 1979: 'The British people are convinced, as we believe, that it is time for a new beginning,' he said. 'So our strategy to check Britain's long-term decline, which has gathered pace in the last five years, is

based on four principles.' The Chancellor went on to list these four principles as follows:

- to strengthen incentives by allowing people to keep more of what they earn, so that hard work, talent and ability are properly rewarded;
- to enlarge freedom of choice for the individual by reducing the role of the state;
- to reduce the burden of financing the public sector, so as to leave room for commerce and industry to prosper;
- to ensure, so far as is possible, that those who take part in collective bargaining understand the consequences of their actions (for that is the way to promote a proper sense of responsibility).

The Chancellor then added the following comment:

> 'These are simple principles, but they require substantial changes in the way our economy is allowed to work. . . . But they will not themselves be enough unless we also squeeze inflation out of the system. It is crucially important to re-establish sound money. We intend to achieve this through firm monetary discipline and fiscal policies consistent with it, including strict control over public expenditure.'

It is convenient, without departing from Sir Geoffrey's scheme too much, to examine Mrs Thatcher's economics in a slightly different order.

Mrs Thatcher's economics

I shall start with the purely *macroeconomic* aspects of economic policy, namely the goal of controlling and eventually eliminating inflation, principally though the control of the money supply. I then move on to an area that has *both macro- and microeconomic facets*: the policy of reducing the size and influence of the public sector.

The use of tax reductions as a means of improving incentives – that part of Mrs Thatcher's economic philosophy which is very much concerned with the supply side of the economy – comes next. Finally I look at another area that is essentially microeconomic – the introduction of legislation both to curb the power of the trades unions and to improve the efficiency of the labour market.

These four elements of economic policy – monetarism and the control of inflation, reining back the public sector, tax cuts on the supply side, and union law and the labour market – make up Mrs Thatcher's economics for the purposes of this book.

Chapter Two

Monetarism and the control of inflation

'Under Labour prices have risen faster than at any peacetime period in the three centuries in which records have been kept, and inflation is now accelerating again. The pound today is worth less than half its 1974 value. On present form it would be halved in value yet again within eight years. Inflation on this scale has come near to destroying our political and social stability. . . . To master inflation, proper monetary discipline is essential, with publicly stated targets for the rate of growth of the money supply. At the same time, a gradual reduction in the size of the Government's borrowing requirement is also vital.' Conservative party manifesto, 1979

The belief that the key to controlling the rate at which prices rise in the economy lies in the control of the amount of money in circulation is based on one of the oldest ideas in economics. The **quantity theory of money** originated almost 300 years ago with John Locke and David Hume. It was mondernized and refined by the modern quantity theorists, or **monetarists,** led by Professor Milton Friedman of the University of Chicago.

The quantity theory of money
In the eighteenth and nineteenth centuries, when the industrialized countries were gradually developing sophisticated banking systems and the use of paper currencies, the belief that prices could not rise without a prior increase in the quantity of money in circulation was the conventional view. It was not until the eve of the First World War, and the beginning of the end of the principle that all paper currencies were backed by gold, that the quantity theory was set down in a form recognizable to modern economists.

The Fisher equation
In 1911, Professor Irving Fisher of Yale University set down the following equation:

$$MV = PT,$$

where M is the quantity of *money* in the economy, V is the number of times it changes hands in a given period, or its **velocity of circulation**, P is the *price* level, and T is the number of *transactions*, again within a given period.

At first glance the equation seems to be indisputable: the quantity of money multiplied by the number of times that money is used to buy goods is just another way of describing the price of goods multiplied by the number sold. There is no way in which, barring leakages into and out of the economy, the two sides of the equation cannot be equal.

But V and T are strange animals. How do we know what they are? The answer, according to Fisher, was that the number of times money changes hands, V, was determined by factors such as the structure of the banking system and the frequency with which people are paid. It could be assumed to change very slowly, if at all.

Similarly, most pre-First World War economists did not feature unemployment in their scheme of things. Any surplus of labour would automatically be corrected by a fall in wages. It followed that, in conditions of **full employment**, the number of transactions was broadly constant over time.

This left the two remaining elements of the equation, M and P, which did change. Further, the quantity theorists thought it only sensible that changes in the quantity of money came before price changes: M determined P, or *increases in the quantity of money led to inflation*.

The Cambridge version

The Fisher equation left the quantity theory open to the charge that it did not prove that the link was from money to prices, and not vice versa. Could not rising prices call forth an increase in the quantity of money in a modern economy as people, realizing that goods were going to cost them more, increased their borrowing from the banks?

This criticism was tackled directly in the **Cambridge cash balance approach** to the quantity theory. This had M and P as before, but introduced two new concepts. The first, in place of T, was Y – the **national income** of the economy in real terms. National income, the sum of incomes in the economy, is equivalent to the amount of expenditure, or transactions. It is also equivalent to the amount of goods produced. Y is a wider concept than T, and easier to grasp.

The Cambridge economists believed that individuals wished to hold a certain proportion of their income in cash. This proportion they called k. Now, if there is a sudden increase in the amount of money in circulation, people have more money than they wish to hold. They go out and spend. Under the classical assumption that real national income is at its full employment level, the effect of an increase in money is an increase in prices.

The Cambridge cash balance version of the quantity theory can be expressed as:

$$M = k\text{PY},$$

where M is the quantity of money in circulation, k is the proportion of income people wish to hold in cash, P is the price level and Y real national income. And the mechanism logically ran from money to prices.

Friedman's modern quantity theory

Finally, in the 1950s, Professor Milton Friedman further refined the quantity theory, and rehabilitated it after it had been discredited in the revolution in economic thinking led by John Maynard Keynes in the 1930s.

Keynes had said that the Cambridge view that people wish to hold a constant proportion of their income in cash was wrong, because the **demand for money** would vary according to the rate of interest. He postulated a speculative demand for money which was very sensitive to interest rates.

Friedman accepted that there were alternative assets that people might hold, and the interest-earning bonds cited by Keynes would be among them. He pointed out, however, that there was a far wider range of these assets than Keynes had allowed, including washing machines and houses.

The effect of an increase in money in circulation would be that people would start off with a lot of cash but would then move some of that cash into other assets – and not just financial assets such as bonds, but also goods. Thus the link from an increase in money to greater spending on goods, while slightly less direct, was as well established as in the Cambridge approach.

In Friedman's view, all the factors that made up the demand for money, including the rate of interest and the relative attractions of buying and owning goods, would tend to cancel each other out, leaving a stable demand for money.

'Stable demand for money' means the same as 'stable velocity of circulation', and this gives us the modern quantity theory of money:

$$MV = PY$$

where M is the stock of money, V is the income velocity of circulation (or the number of times a given amount of money changes hands as someone's income), P is the price level, and Y is real national income.

Unlike his predecessors, Friedman did not suggest that Y was unchanged at the full employment level of national income; when the stock of money changes, he said, it produces changes in both national income and prices. But the larger the increase in the stock of money, the more likely were its effects to show up in higher prices rather than higher economic growth. Friedman wrote in 1956:

> 'There is perhaps no other empirical relation in economics that has been observed to recur so uniformly under so wide a variety of circumstances as the relation between substantial changes in the stock of money and in prices; the one is invariably linked to the other and in the same direction; this uniformity is, I suspect, of the same order as many of the uniformities that form the basis of the physical sciences.'

The quantity theory in practice

When policy-makers take $MV = PY$ as their basis, then the conduct of policy appears to be very straightforward. Suppose that the economy is growing by 3 per cent a year (in other words Y is rising by 3 per cent annually) but that inflation, the rate of change of the price level P, is an unacceptable 10 per cent. To reduce inflation to perhaps 5 per cent, action has to be taken to reduce the rate of growth of the money stock. In the case outlined above, the prescription would be to reduce the rise in the **money supply** from an existing rate of 13 per cent to something near to 8 per cent.

On the face of it this could hardly be simpler: set your target for the money supply and everything else falls into place. In practice, of course, things are rarely so simple.

What is money?

This sounds like a question hardly worth asking. But think about it for a moment: money is obviously the cash that you carry around in your pockets, but it is a lot of other things as well.

In a modern, credit economy, most people would take money to include cheques drawn on banks or building societies. They would also include overdraft facilities – automatic entitlements to borrow – including company overdrafts. And no modern definition of money, at least from the consumer's point of view, could possibly exclude those flexible friends, the plastic credit cards.

In Britain, at present, the Bank of England publishes statistics for a range of definitions of money, running from M0 through to M5. M0 is a **narrow money** measure, comprising notes and coins and balances held by the commercial banks at the Bank of England. It is therefore close to traditional definitions of money. M5 includes, as well as notes and coins, many other things, the most important of which are accounts held by people at banks and building societies. It is a **broad money** measure.

How do you control money?
There is more to money than the cash we carry around with us, and so there has to be more involved in controlling it than simply regulating the machines at the Royal Mint.

Monetary policy – that part of economic policy concerned with the availability of money and credit in the economy – has to try to do more than influence the number of £5 notes we carry in our wallets or purses; it has also to bear down upon the rate at which we write cheques or use our credit cards. (Fiscal policy, the other leg to economic policy concerned with taxation and public expenditure, is dealt with later in the book.)

Governments can seek to control the rate of growth of money and credit directly. **Credit controls** on 'hire purchase' were one example of this; the Supplementary Special Deposits Scheme, usually known as the **corset**, was another. (The latter restricted the rate at which the banks could increase their lending.) Both were abolished by Mrs Thatcher's government. Under present (1988) arrangements, the main way in which money and credit are controlled is through their price. The growth of money is controlled through the level of interest rates, as well as by the Government's influence on confidence and expectations in the economy.

As we shall see, controlling money with such a limited range of weapons is far from easy.

Will velocity be constant?
The essential assumption of practical monetarism is that the demand for money – and therefore the velocity of circulation – will be constant or move in a predictable way. If we think back to $MV = PY$, we can see what happens if V is not constant.

Suppose that, at the time the government is trying to achieve a reduction in inflation by slowing down the money supply, there is an increase in the velocity of circulation – each unit of money changes hands more frequently. It is easy to see why economic policy would be thwarted. The reduction in the rate of growth of M is compensated for by an increase in V. PY is left unchanged.

In the opposite situation, where the government is trying to ease

7

monetary conditions by letting the money supply grow faster, in order to boost the economy, a reduction in the velocity of circulation would again upset things. The desired aim of increasing PY would be thwarted.

The stability or otherwise of the demand for money and velocity of circulation has been one of the battlegrounds between the Keynesian economists (the followers of Keynes) and the monetarists.

The Keynesians argued that demand and velocity were will-o'-the-wisps which shifted around frequently. The monetarists argued the case for stable and predictable money demand and velocity. Much of the hard evidence – and the experience of governments who have attempted to put monetarism into practice – suggests that the velocity of circulation is not stable.

This may not be too much of a problem, of course, if velocity is moving in a predictable way. This, too, does not often appear to be the case.

What about the real economy?

In the example outlined earlier of how a government would go about reducing the rate of inflation from 10 to 5 per cent by reducing money supply growth, it was assumed that this process would have no effect on the growth of real national income, which held steady at 3 per cent.

A tightening of monetary policy might, however, hit the real economy as much as it affected inflation. In the worst case, the reduction in the rate of growth of money from 13 to 8 per cent, as in the example, could leave inflation unchanged at 10 per cent and entirely impact on the real economy – turning growth of 3 per cent into recession where the economy is contracting by 2 per cent.

Monetarists recognized this possiblity, although few were prepared for the dramatic economic slowdown that marked the earlier years of Mrs Thatcher's experiment with monetarism. Professor Milton Friedman gave evidence in 1980 to the Treasury and Civil Service Committee, a House of Commons committee which was conducting a special examination of monetary policy. He said:

> 'A successful policy of reducing inflation will have as an unavoidable side effect a temporary retardation in economic growth. However, continuation of the present level of inflation, and even more further acceleration of inflation, would at best postpone the retardation at the expense of a more severe retardation later.
>
> 'Past mistakes in economic policy have left us with no soft options. Our only real alternatives are to accept a temporary economic slowdown now

as part of a programme for ending inflation, or to experience a more severe slowdown somewhat later as a result of continued or accelerated inflation.'

Timing problems

Monetarists have never claimed that the relationship between money and prices is a perfectly predictable one. Instead, there are said to be 'long and variable lags' between changes in the rate of growth of money and changes in economic growth and inflation (the gross domestic product in money terms).

Friedman, for example, found that the average **time lag** between peaks in the growth of money and peaks in economic activity was 16 months, but that this average was within a range from 6 to 29 months. In the opposite situation, a low point in money growth came, on average, 12 months ahead of a low point in economic activity. But here again the range was wide, from 4 to 22 months.

Therefore, monetarism could never be used with precision. Governments could not use monetarism for '**fine tuning**' the economy. This is why Friedman and other monetarists said that governments should adopt firm rules for the rate of growth of money, stick to them and, with a little patience, the beneficial results should come through. Clearly, this is easier for a theoretician to say than for a politician to accept.

Mrs Thatcher's monetarism

Mrs Thatcher's first government (in 1979) was not the first in Britain to operate targets for the money supply. Labour governments in the late 1960s and in the period 1976–79 had also sought to control the money supply within targets, at the insistence of the International Monetary Fund in Washington.

There have been three distinct phases to the monetarist experiment in Britain under Mrs Thatcher, beginning with something close to a textbook version of the theory, and gradually moving away from that.

Phase one: Rigid targets and the medium-term financial strategy

Mrs Thatcher's first government, unlike its predecessors, was ideologically committed to monetarism. Ministers believed not only that control of the money supply would squeeze inflation out of the system, but also that by publicly announcing **monetary targets** for the rate of growth of the money stock they would influence **inflationary expectations** in the economy, particularly in the crucial area of wage

9

bargaining. This intention was set out clearly by the Treasury in its March 1980 Budget document:

> 'Control of the money supply will over a period of years reduce the rate of inflation. The speed with which inflation falls will depend crucially on expectations both within the United Kingdom and overseas. It is to provide a· firm basis for those expectations that the government has announced its firm commitment ot a progressive reduction in money supply growth.'

The measure of money which the government chose to target was called **sterling M3**. It consisted of notes and coins and all sterling sight and time deposits with the banks, plus sterling certificates of deposit. The main elements within sterling M3 (now called plain M3) were cash and bank deposits. **Sight deposits** are those which are withdraw-able on demand (in other words current accounts). **Time deposits** are those where notice has to be given to withdraw, or an interest penalty incurred, and are more generally known as deposit accounts. Sterling M3 was at the broad end of the spectrum of measures of money, described earlier.

In the first Budget of the Thatcher government, in June 1979, a one-year target was set for the growth of sterling M3. But the following March, with the launch of the **medium-term financial strategy**, a more ambitious four-year programme was set out, as shown in Table 1.

Table 1 The medium-term financial strategy

	1980–81	1981–82	1982–83	1983–84
Target growth rate sterling M3 (%)	7–11	6–10	5–9	4–8
Actual growth rate (%)	17.9	13.6	11.7	8.2

The aim was to bring down the *rate of growth* of sterling M3 within a target range fixed for each financial year (the government's financial year runs from April to April). As the second line in the table shows, a reduction in sterling M3 growth was achieved, but the original targets were never actually hit.

The effect of the attempt to reduce money supply growth was, initially, to bring about the most severe British economic recession since the 1930s. This was not necessarily because the monetary targets were too tight – and even if they were the targets were not met.

Rather, it was because of these two accompanying factors:

- the failure of wage settlements to come down quickly enough
- the sharp rise in the pound which was an important effect of the attempt to control the money supply.

The pay boom
The more slowly that expectations adjust in the economy to the idea of lower inflation, the greater the effect that controlling the money supply (M) is likely to have on real national income (Y) rather than on the price level (P).

In 1979 and 1980, when pay settlements should ideally have been moving sharply lower in line with the government's firm anti-inflationary resolve, they instead moved sharply higher. There were several reasons, some the fault of the government, some not.

As a backdrop, the Iranian revolution late in 1978 had produced the second sharp rise in world oil prices in a decade. This added to inflation and wage pressures in the UK.

Then, in the run-up to the 1979 General Election in May, Mrs Thatcher promised to honour the recommendations of a special commission set up to examine *public sector pay*. The Comparability Commission on Public Sector Pay, under Professor Hugh Clegg, recommended big increases, notably for low-paid workers in the public sector, and these set the tone for the 1979–80 wage round.

The June Budget (of which more later) then included a big increase in value-added tax (VAT), from rates of 8 and 12.5 per cent to a uniform 15 per cent. In addition, the Budget ushered in a period of high interest rates, which pushed mortgage rates up. Both produced a sharp increase in inflation, measured by the **retail price index**, and this added to wage demands.

The government's stated aim of achieving a progressive reduction in money supply growth had little impact on wage bargainers. Trades union officials did not attach any credence to the government's monetary targets and carried on as before, for a time.

The strong pound
Most textbook monetarism was concerned with the theoretical world of the closed economy, with no complications like overseas trade and the exchange rate. In 1979 and 1980 interest rates were pushed sharply higher to rein back the growth of the target money supply measure, sterling M3.

The effect of this, in combination with the boost provided by higher oil prices (because of North Sea oil the pound was now a **petro-currency**), was to push the pound sharply higher. In 1980–81 the pound reached the heights of $2.40–2.50 against the dollar, compared with a low point of just above $1.50 in the mid-1970s.

These factors, coupled with high wage settlements at home, made it virtually impossible for many British firms to compete either in domestic or in export markets.

Deep recession

The side effects of the initial monetarist experiment were dramatic. The economy fell into the deepest recession since the 1930s. Manufacturing output slumped 17.5 per cent between June 1979 and the spring of 1981. Unemployment rose to 3 million during 1982, from 1.2 million in 1979. It was in this context that the government embarked on the second phase of the British monetarist experiment.

Phase two: Pragmatic monetarism

When the government reviewed its record on the economy after two years in power, it was clear that the monetarist strategy, based on sterling M3, had run into difficulties. A new model was needed which would avoid the worst of the old and, in particular, the over-valued exchange rate.

The new model, formally launched in March 1982, was a reworked medium-term financial strategy. As well as setting targets for sterling M3, the government now brought in a narrow money measure, M1 (consisting mainly of notes and coins and bank current accounts), as well as a wider measure, PSL (private sector liquidity) 2, which was even broader than sterling M3, and included some building society accounts.

The old monetary targets were scrapped and new ones put in their place: 8–12 per cent for 1982–83, instead of 5–9 per cent, falling gradually to 6–10 per cent by 1984–85.

The tone of monetary policy shifted. No longer would everything be sacrificed in favour of hitting one particular target. Instead, policy would be conducted with rather more discretion than had been the case initially. A Bank of England official, John Fforde, described this change in 1982:

> 'As may now be visible, this means that setting objectives for the money supply, and endeavouring to carry them out, has become a more humble pursuit. It does not lack resolve, or a clear sense of direction, but it recognizes once more that the successful execution of monetary policy

requires the exercise of judgement, and of a constantly interpretative approach to the evolving pattern of evidence. Except in some grave emergency, or in the initial phase of a novel strategy, the abandonment of judgement in favour of some simple, rigid, quantitative rule about the money supply does not reliably deliver acceptable results.'

Phase three: Pragmatism

The second phase of monetary policy lasted until January 1985, when the second of two sterling crises in six months had pushed the pound to within a whisker of one-to-one parity with the dollar. There was then a further policy shift.

In October 1985, sterling M3 was temporarily abandoned as a target. It was brought back in 1986 but finally abandoned completely in 1987. In March 1988, the Treasury said that more attention would be paid to the wider M4 measure than to M3. M4 includes building society as well as bank deposits. But the only money target was for the narrow money measure M0, and it was clear that domestic monetary targets would take second place to the exchange rate in the conduct of policy.

It was back to the familiar model of monetary policy of the 1950s and 60s, when interest rates were raised or lowered according to the strength of the pound. And it was no longer economic policy according to the quantity theory of money.

In October 1987 Nigel Lawson, Chancellor of the Exchequer since 1983, called (in a speech to the International Monetary Fund) for a permanent system of managed exchange rates for the major currencies. The replacement of monetary targets by exchange rate targets was almost complete.

Why did inflation fall?

Britain's inflation rate, which reached 25 per cent in the mid 1970s and over 20 per cent in the early 1980s, averaged between 4 and 5 per cent in the period 1983 to 1987.

The description above suggests that the experience of Mrs Thatcher's governments with monetarism was of missed targets followed by a gradual shift away from rigid ideas about targeting the money supply. It does not read like an obvious success story, so why did inflation fall? There are several possible explanations.

Firstly, low inflation rates were achieved in the 1950s and 1960s without monetary targets. There is no reason to credit monetarism with that earlier success except insofar as the need to preserve fixed exchange rates (under the **Bretton Woods system** which lasted until

1973) may have exerted discipline in monetary policy. Low inflation occurred without monetarism then, so why not now?

Secondly, the two great inflationary surges of recent years – in the mid 1970s and around 1980 – followed sharp rises in world oil prices. For most of the 1980s oil and commodity prices have been weak (the price of oil fell briefly to less than $10 a barrel in 1986) and this weakness has exerted a downward influence on inflation.

Thirdly, recession and high unemployment have had a restraining influence on wage pressure in the major economies, although not enough to make major inroads into high unemployment levels.

Finally, fiscal policy – taxation and public expenditure – has been tightened in Britain, and in most other countries excepting the United States. Keynesian economists would say that this has been at least as important in producing low inflation as has monetary policy.

KEY WORDS

Quantity theory of money	Corset
Monetarists	Time lag
Fisher equation	Fine tuning
Velocity of circulation	Monetary targets
Full employment	Inflationary expectations
Cambridge cash balance	Sterling M3
approach	Sight deposits
National income	Time deposits
Demand for money	Medium-term financial
Money supply	strategy
Narrow money	Retail price index
Broad money	Petro-currency
Monetary policy	Bretton Woods system
Credit controls	

Reading list

Bain, A.D., *The Economics of the Financial System*, Martin Robertson, 1981.

Lewis, Mervyn, 'Rethinking monetary policy', *Lloyds Bank Review*, July 1980.

Keegan, William, *Mrs Thatcher's Economic Experiment*, Penguin, 1984.

Smith, David, *The Rise and Fall of Monetarism*, Penguin, 1987.

Essay Topics

1. 'The quantity theory of money has little relevance for present-day economic policy.' Discuss with reference to economic policy in Britain since 1979.

2. Keynesian economists regard the demand for money and the velocity of circulation as 'will-o'-the-wisps'. What do they mean by this and, if it is true, what problems does it create for governments seeking to stabilize the economy by regulating the growth of the money supply?

3. 'A successful policy of reducing inflation will have as an unavoidable side effect a temporary retardation in economic growth' (Milton Friedman). Explain, with reference to the quantity theory of money, how this can come about. Why was the 'temporary retardation' so severe in Britain between 1979 and 1981?

4. 'It is to provide a firm basis for (inflationary) expectations that the government has announced its firm commitment to a progressive reduction in money supply growth' (1980 Financial Statement and Budget Report). Did the announcement of monetary targets in Britain reduce inflationary expectations? Discuss with reference to the sharp rise in unemployment between 1979 and 1982.

5. 'Monetarism must have worked because inflation fell in the 1980s.' Discuss.

6. 'The successful execution of monetary policy requires the exercise of judgement, and of a constantly interpretative approach to the evolving pattern of evidence' (John Fforde). Examine this statement with reference to the development of monetary policy in Britain since 1979.

7. 'The exchange rate is the most important monetary target.' Discuss, drawing out both the similarities and the differences between present economic policy and the period until 1973, when exchange rates were fixed.

8. Describe the quantity theory of money and its development. How did the breakdown of the 'classical' assumption of full employment affect the quantity theory?

Data Response Question 1
Monetary trends

Read the two extracts from the February 1988 Bank of England *Quarterly Bulletin*.

1. What was the main reason for the strong growth in M0?
2. What was the target range for M0, and how did it perform in relation to this range?
3. Intervention – official action by the Bank of England to restrain the pound – could have been expected to expand broad money growth. What offsetting factors meant that it did not do so?
4. The public sector borrowing requirement is described as being in surplus. How would you expect the BP sale to contribute to this?
5. What did the Bank cite as the main reason for strong broad money growth?
6. What was the main purpose of the rise in personal sector borrowing?
7. What were the specific reasons mentioned for the strength of private sector credit demand in relation to the strength of the real economy?
8. What contributed to the fall in the 12-month rate of growth of M0?
9. What effect did the fall in equity prices have on broad money?
10. Why did M4 continue to grow more slowly than M3 in spite of strong inflows into building societies from persons.

Monetary developments add to the impression of strong domestic demand

Monetary growth remains strong. M0, no doubt reflecting the buoyancy of consumer spending, grew strongly in the second half of last year, though the twelve-month increase remained within the 2%–6% target range. The various measures of broad money, too, continued to grow rapidly. Intervention contributed to changes in the month-to-month growth of broad money. However, over the last three months for which figures are available, taken together the impact of intervention on money has been largely matched by a combination of funding and a PSBR surplus, in part representing the sale of BP shares. Broad money growth, therefore, has reflected the strength of credit demand from the private sector, which remained at the high level of the summer months. Only part of this can be attributed to personal sector borrowing, particularly mortgage borrowing, while the profile of demand through the year has been similar to last year, but with the banks taking a bigger market share. The remainder reflects other aspects of the strength of the real economy, for example, substantial stockbuilding, as well as position-taking associated with takeover and merger activity which persisted even after the stock market fall.

Monetary aggregates and credit

The figures in this section are seasonally adjusted except for twelve-month growth rates or as otherwise stated.

Over the three months to December, M0 growth, although slower than in the third quarter, was again high at 1.8%, but the twelve-month growth rate fell from 5.2% to 4.2%: in part this fall reflected erratic fluctuations in bankers' balances, and the growth rate of notes and coin showed a more modest fall. The growth of broad money within the quarter was little changed from the previous three months, although the twelve-month growth rates of M3 and M4 increased to 22.8% and 16.3% respectively from 19.5% and 14.9%. The falls in equity prices had some impact on broad money by provoking increased retail inflows into building societies but it is, as yet, difficult to gauge the impact of these price movements on growth of broad money as a whole. M4 continued to grow more slowly than M3 despite the strong inflows into building societies from persons, the effect of which on M4 was offset by an increase in the societies' holdings of bank deposits.

Data Response Question 2
Interest rate changes

Read the accompanying article from *The Times* of 11 March 1987.

1. Describe the annual interest rate cycle.
2. Is it a precise mechanism?
3. What do foreign exchange dealers expect in January?
4. Why do market operators expect interest rate cuts around the time of the Budget?
5. When are money market pressures at their most intense, and why?
6. Why should January and February normally be associated with sterling strength?
7. Why has this not been the case in recent years?
8. When is the easiest time for the authorities to sell gilt-edged stock?
9. What is the Grand Old Duke of York syndrome?
10. Why is the Bank of England unwilling to accept the notion of seasonal movements in exchange rates and interest rates?

Why base rates rise and fall with the seasons

There has been a certain familiarity about this week's interest rate developments. If it is March, base rates must be coming down.

The reduction in base rates from 11 to 10.5 per cent will almost certainly be followed by another cut next week. No one can accuse the Treasury and the Bank of England of taking risks by allowing the banks to trim their rates.

It is a far cry from the situation just a few months ago, when the Chancellor of the Exchequer held off from raising rates until after the Conservative Party conference and then faced a nervous run-up to Christmas as the markets bayed for further interest-rate rises.

Why has the situation changed so dramatically? Has the monetary situation improved that much in a short time? Or is it that interest rates display a seasonal pattern?

Since the early 1980s, base rates have moved within something like an annual cycle. The cycle is far from precise but it suggests interest rate changes do not occur at random.

Interest rates tend to be high around the turn of the year, falling through the spring months – hence the profusion of Budget-time base rate cuts – and flat to slightly firmer over the summer months.

In some years, this slight firmness during the summer has been rather more pronounced, as in the case of July 1984, when interest rates were raised sharply to defend sterling. Indeed, before the 1980s, July tended to be a month when sterling was particularly prone to weakness, as evidensed by a succession of emergency July packages to protect the pound.

Rates tend to be soft in the autumn, particularly during the party conference season. This is followed by a tendency to rise as winter starts.

There are several reasons why interest rates may be expected to move with the seasons. The first has to do with market operators.

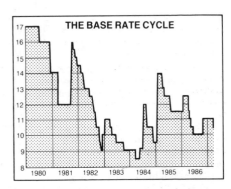

THE BASE RATE CYCLE

If people expect certain changes to occur at certain times, then those expectations can become self-fulfilling. Thus, foreign exchange dealers prepare themselves for an assault on sterling in January, and the money markets to test the Bank of England on its willingness to allow rate rises.

Chancellors, it is correctly believed in the markets, like to see their Budgets receive the accolade of an interest rate cut. Again, once this is built into expectations, it can happen almost automatically. The same is true of rate cuts in the party conference season.

But expectations alone may not be enough to force changes in rates. And expectations can be wrong. This January, for example, there was no sterling in-spired raising of interest rates.

During the year, the Bank of England has to accommodate varying pressures in the money markets. These pressures are at their most intense during the corporate tax-paying season from the middle of December until February.

During this period, large shortages develop in the money markets, shortages which, as a matter of course, the Bank takes out through its money market operations.

There is no reason why large money market shortages should be translated into higher base rates.

However, if big daily shortages in the money markets occur in tandem with other pressures for interest rate changes, – for example those coming through the exchange rate – then avoiding base rate changes is more difficult for the authorities. The bigger the run of daily shortages, the harder it is for the authorities to prevent the money markets forcing a base rate change.

Against this, there is the traditional reason why January-February should be associated with sterling strength and, therefore, an easier tone for interest rates.

British companies with overseas subsidiaries repatriate funds at this time to pay their tax bills and this flow of funds across the exchanges ought to provide sterling with a boost.

But such flows, in recent years, may have been offset by the movement abroad of profits by foreign companies operating in the North Sea and, more generally, by the importance of very short-term capital flows in determining exchange rates.

North Sea oil should have transformed the seasonality of both sterling and interest rates more than it has. The second quarter of the year has frequently been a period of oil price weakness, reflecting the annual low point in demand.

But this has not been carried through to pressure on the exchange rate and interest rates. In fact, the second quarter has typically been a period of sterling strength and interest rate falls.

One reason for the interest rate declines has to do with the cash flow of financial institutions. The peak months for dividend receipts by the institutions are January, May and November. Selling gilt-edged stock should be relatively easy for the authorities in these months but, in the intervening months, gilt sales may have to be teased out by providing the market with regular small interest rate cuts.

This phenomenon, usually known as the Grand Old Duke of York syndrome, suggests more official control over interest rates than is, in fact, possible. But it provides a rationale, certainly, for spring-time base rate cuts.

The Treasury's own work on seasonal movements in the exchange rate and, for that matter, interest rates, suggests that any seasonality falls short of being statistically significant. The Bank of England has been unwilling to accept the principle of seasonal movements in exchange rates or interest rates.

The problem for the monetary authority in accepting the view that part of any movement in, say, sterling, simply reflected seasonal behaviour, is that it would imply allowing the pound to fall in January, for example, in the certain knowledge that any weakness would disappear by March.

It is the case that in recent years, with the notable exception of 1985, base rates have mainly ended the first quarter at a lower level than they started it. It is also the case that after the March flurry of base rate cuts, progress in the second quarter is usually slow, and a fall of more than 1 per cent over the quarter would be unusual notwithstanding election timing.

One thing is certain: whatever the changes in base rates through the year, seasonally adjusted, interest rates are too high.

David Smith
Economics Correspondent

Chapter Three

Reining back the public sector

'The state takes too much of the nation's income; its share must be steadily reduced. When it spends and borrows too much, taxes, prices and unemployment rise so that in the long run there is less wealth with which to improve our standard of living and our social services.' Conservative party manifesto, 1979

What is the right size for the public sector?

The term **public sector** is used so frequently that it seems hardly worth defining; but let us be clear what we are concerned with. The public sector consists of:

- all the people required to run government at both national and local level, and the resources at the disposal of those people;
- those services that are paid for out of taxation, including state education, the National Health Service, the police and the armed forces;
- the land and buildings owned by the government (public sector assets);
- state industries, whether or not they generate a profit.

Another way of distinguishing between public and private sectors is to draw the distinction between market and non-market activities. Government departments, state industries and the National Health Service are all in varying degrees insulated from the pressures of the market in a way that the bulk of private industry, for example, is not.

In the 1987–88 financial year, general government expenditure was intended to be just under 43 per cent of the country's gross domestic product, similar to the level inherited by Mrs Thatcher in 1979. In the intervening period, government spending rose and then fell as a proportion of gross domestic product (see Figure 1). The government regards 43 per cent as too large a share and intends to reduce it to just above 41 per cent by 1989–90.

The difficulty is that there are no hard and fast rules about the right size for the public sector in a mixed economy such as that of Britain. (We call it a **mixed economy** because it consists of both public and

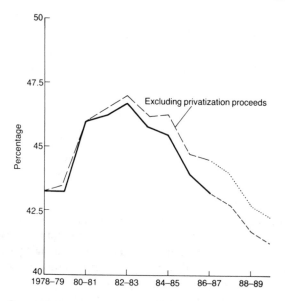

Figure 1 General government expenditure as a percentage of GDP (Public Expenditure White Paper, 1987, Part One)

private sectors – it is neither 100 per cent free enterprise nor 100 per cent state-run.)

In the mid-1970s, official figures were produced suggesting that public expenditure was equivalent to 60 per cent of Britain's gross domestic product. Warnings were sounded that a public sector of this size threatened not only the economic well-being of the country but her political and social stability. As it turned out the figures were misleading, involving elements of double counting: the actual figure was below 50 per cent. But the episode brought out deep-seated fears – even in a country with a well-developed welfare state – of too big a state sector. And the Thatcher government was able to advance a number of arguments for reining back the public sector.

Crowding out

The idea of crowding out had its ancestry in the so-called Treasury view of the 1920s and 30s, when successive British governments rejected the early ideas of Keynes about boosting public spending in order to reduce unemployment. Any increase in spending would require additional government borrowing, it was said. The pressure of such borrowing would push up interest rates and penalize private industry. The expansion of the public sector would thus be accompanied by a contraction in the private sector. The economy as a whole, and unemployment in particular, would be no better off.

Post-war economists refined this view into two distinct types of crowding out.

Resource crowding out

The resources of the economy are the factors of production – land, labour and capital – together with, according to the old classical economists, entrepreneurial ability. These resources are scarce. It follows that the greater the share of them taken up by the public sector, the less is available for the private sector.

One common reason advanced for Britain's long-run industrial decline was that the best talent from the schools and universities went, not into manufacturing industry where the financial rewards were often lower and the work less satisfying, but into the civil service. This was an example of resource crowding out.

Economists have criticized the use of the concept of resource crowding out when there are clearly unused resources in the economy – as, for example, at times of high unemployment. Even in such situations, though, it is still possible for there to be a limited supply of labour with certain skills. Even so, the reduction in the size of the civil service under Mrs Thatcher, and a perceived decline in the attractiveness of working in the public sector, have not solved manufacturing industry's problem. Now it loses much of the best young talent to the City and other private sector service occupations.

Financial crowding out

Advocates of the crowding out hypothesis would concede that there are certain situations when the scope for resource crowding out is limited; but, they would argue, *financial* crowding out can occur in a wider variety of situations.

Suppose that the government embarks on a programme of public expenditure which increases its annual borrowing (the **public sector borrowing requirement**) from £10 billion to £20 billion. The effect is to increase the amount of borrowing, whatever the rate of interest, by £10 billion. In Figure 2 the government's additional borrowing produces an outward shift in the demand for funds from D_1 to D_2. The effect, with the supply curve for funds unchanged (S), is to raise interest rates from R_1 to R_2, and to increase the amount borrowed from Q_1 to Q_2.

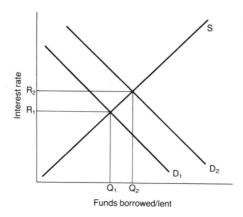

Figure 2 Borrowing and interest rates

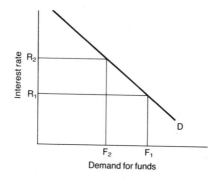

Figure 3 The private sector's demand for funds

Now consider for a moment the private sector's demand for funds, as shown in Figure 3. The rise in interest rates from R_1 to R_2 would reduce the amount of funds demanded by the private sector – it would reduce private sector borrowing from F_1 to F_2. So it is possible that, if the extra borrowing by the public sector is exactly matched by reduced private sector borrowing, we would be back to our original demand schedule D_1 in Figure 2, with the important difference that a greater share of borrowing is by the public sector.

Critics of the financial crowding out argument say that the central idea of a finite amount of funds being available is not realistic. They also say that the rate of interest is only one of a number of factors determining private borrowing, and that raising interest rates has not proved to be an effective way of restraining borrowing. Companies

23

borrow when they see investment opportunities, individuals when they are determined to purchase a house or consumer good.

There have been occasions, however, when big increases in public borrowing have affected the interest rate *climate*, making it more difficult for private companies to raise finance in the City. And it is the case that around 80 per cent of daily stock exchange turnover is in government stocks (or **gilts** as they are more popularly known).

Public sector inefficiency

Even without resorting to the crowding out concept, free market economists can put forward a strong case for cutting back the public sector. The starting point for the argument is that the market exerts competitive pressures, which require economic units (firms) to operate efficiently. Without such competitive pressures there is no spur to efficiency. Hence the public sector, it is argued, will always tend to be less efficient than the private sector.

In the private sector, or at least an ideal model of it, spurs to efficiency work in a number of ways. Owners, managers and the workforce know that if they do not produce the right goods at the right price the firm will go out of business and they will lose their jobs. Managers are spurred on by the need to make profits; workers by the fact that the harder they work, the more they will get paid. Productivity is encouraged, waste is penalized, bureaucratic inefficiency is unforgiveable.

In the public sector, things are different. The public sector body is the monopoly supplier of a particular good or service. The customer has to take what is offered because there is no alternative. There is job security for managers and the workforce. Even if the organization does badly it will not go out of business. Managers have insufficient reason to strive for greater efficiency because there is no reward for doing so – why rock the boat? Workers are paid the same, however hard they work. The scope for productivity gains is limited, the reward for such gains non-existent. Waste is not penalized, bureaucratic inefficiency is the norm.

Readers may have noticed that the above descriptions of the public and private sectors are caricatures. There are many private firms where the profit motive fails to permeate through to middle managers, and where the workforce does not link poor performance to the threat to job security. In the public sector, increased accountability and performance targets have allowed state bodies to match or improve upon private sector performance.

But the caricature is one that is widely believed, and the Conservative party had little difficulty selling it to the public.

Evidence for public and private sector efficiency

Comparisons of public and private sector performance are notoriously difficult. There is often little overlap between the services offered in the two. Where there is, one has to be sure that like is being compared with like.

Consider the National Health Service and private medicine. Private hospitals can offer an efficient service in conducting certain operations, without the problem of long waiting lists and bed shortages which are prevalent in the National Health Service. The NHS, on the other hand, is required to run a comprehensive service, available to all. Private hospitals are involved in only a part of the health-care market – you do not go to a private hospital for casualty treatment after a road accident. Private hospitals cater only for those who have had the foresight to take out private health insurance, or who can afford to pay. A poor, elderly person with a history of medical problems has to settle for the NHS – and it is in the necessary treatment of such patients that the costs of the NHS escalate.

Even without such problems in comparing services, there are still difficulties. All nurses and doctors in Britain are trained in the NHS. Most consultants have as their main job an NHS position. The NHS is generating what economists call **externalities** – wider social benefits – by training and providing the staff employed in private hospitals.

There are many other examples of externalities. Many of the well-paid economists in the City began their careers with the Treasury and the Bank of England. Their value in the private sector is enhanced because, having been involved in economic policy on the inside, they are better placed to assess policy from the outside.

In some cases, governments have required state industries or government departments to produce externalities explicitly by, for example, making them set up in areas of high unemployment. They may be made to lead the way in the employment of the disabled or racial minorities. This may not lead to inefficiency; but if it does it is the consequence of policy and not necessarily of the fact that the organization is in the public sector.

A study carried out by the economist Richard Pryke (consult the reading list) does paint a picture of public sector inefficiency. He analysed the performance of the main nationalized industries over the period 1968 to 1978 and concluded:

'The performance of the nationalized industries over the past decade has ranged from being good in parts – telecommunications and gas – to being almost wholly bad – BSC and postal services. Although the picture is not wholly black, most of the industries display serious inefficiency because they do not use the minimum quantities of labour and capital to produce the goods and services that they provide. Furthermore, resources are being misallocated because of the widespread failure to pursue the optimum policies for pricing and production.'

He later compared the performance of specific parts of the public sector against private sector counterparts. Sealink, then part of British Rail, provided its services at a greater cost than Townsend Thoresen. The gas and electricity showrooms, measured in sales per square foot of floor space, did badly when set against Currys.

Results for other countries have been less clear-cut. In Canada, no significant productivity differences were detected between Canadian National, the public railway operator, and Canadian Pacific, a private firm. Similar inconclusive results emerged from comparisons in the Australian airline industry and US power supply.

Public and private monopolies

One of the commonest criticisms of **privatization** – the government's policy of transferring nationalized industries and other state assets and services to the private sector – is that it achieves nothing unless, in the case of monopolies such as gas and electricity supply, privatization also involves an injection of competition.

Critics of the policy (and British Telecom is the most ciriticized embodiment of that policy) say that **natural monopolies** can only be prevented from abusing their monopoly position when they are in state hands. Ministers can direct monolithic corporations on price, the standard of service, and so on.

The government would counter by saying that a properly regulated private monopoly will always be preferable to a public monopoly. Efficiency is forced upon the private monopoly by the need to perform for shareholders (and in the case of the privatized firms there are plenty of those). Meanwhile, regulatory watchdogs, with sharp teeth that are always ready to bite, provide safeguards against abuse.

Few would deny that the new private monopolies are good at generating profits. Arguments will continue to rage about whether the watchdogs – such as Oftel for British Telecom and Ofgas for British Gas – are effective.

The public sector burden

The greater the size of the public sector, the greater the amount of taxation or government borrowing that is needed to balance it. I shall examine the incentive effects of taxation in Chapter 4. The argument about restricting the size of the public sector to a level which can be met by taxation, without adversely affecting incentives, comes down to the fact that, ultimately, the wealth created in the private sector has to pay for the bulk of the public sector.

In the period 1976–78, the Labour government had to cut back sharply on public expenditure, after calling in the International Monetary Fund (**IMF**). The 1979 Conservative manifesto picked up on this and attacked Labour:

> 'By enlarging the role of the state and diminishing the role of the individual, they have crippled the enterprise and effort on which a prosperous country with improving social service depends.'

We come back to the question of what is the right size for the public sector. Clearly there is no easy answer. Furthermore it is no use specifying a fixed level for public spending as a proportion of gross domestic product for all time: that proportion should vary according to circumstances. Was there a case, for example, for running a larger public sector during the period of maximum production and tax revenues from Britain's North Sea oilfields?

A naturally increasing public sector

I noted earlier that general government expenditure is currently running at about 43 per cent of gross domestic product. Public spending's share of the economy was high at over 45 per cent in the special conditions prevailing immediately after the Second World War. It dropped to more normal peacetime levels of 33–35 per cent in the 1950s, rising steadily to 40 per cent by the end of the 1960s. During the 1970s the share rose to over 45 per cent.

This increase was due to two factors. The first was the deliberate policy of improving public provision of services and, through nationalization, taking firms into public ownership. This was within the general policy context whereby public expenditure was used as a means of ensuring continued economic growth at times when private expenditure was weak.

The second reason related to the natural tendency for the public sector's share of the 'national cake' to increase. In a situation where productivity gains are concentrated in the private sector, the additional resources (wages, investment, etc.) allocated to the private sector will be partly offset by rising output per worker. In the public sector, where productivity gains are lower or impossible to measure, greater provision of services requires proportionately greater resources. Economists call this the **relative price effect,** and it occurs because the cost per unit of output of public services rises faster than that for private services and, therefore, of the overall price level for the economy. It follows that even the same amount of public services will require a rising share of private sector income to be taken up by taxation.

Therefore, governments have to take steps just to stop the public sector from increasing its relative size under its own steam. They have to take painful decisions on cutting public services or increasing public sector efficiency just to stand still in terms of the proportion of national income allocated to the public sector.

Public sector policy in practice – three phases of control

Just as monetary policy under Mrs Thatcher moved through three distinct stages, so a similar development has occurred with public expenditure. The three phases of control were:

- the initial attempt to put into force real (inflation-adjusted) reductions in the overall level of public spending;
- a revised policy of trying to hold public expenditure steady in real terms, implying a sharp fall in the proportion of GDP accounted for by public expenditure – as long as the rest of the economy was growing;
- a third phase which recognized that both the above aims were too ambitious.

Policy in the third phase attempted to ensure that real growth in public spending was below the growth rate in the economy as a whole. This, if successful, implies a gradual fall in public spending as a proportion of GDP.

Phase one: Real cuts

Mrs Thatcher's government was not the first to attempt to cut public expenditure. Governments had periodically resorted to cuts (which were often deferments of planned increases) as part of austerity packages over the years. The most notable example of this was the Labour government in 1976, under the influence of the IMF.

The Conservative government elected in 1979 was the first to aim for systematic real reductions in public expenditure over a period of years. The programme began almost immediately the government was elected and was formalized in the 1980 Public Expenditure White Paper.

The plans included a real increase in spending of just over 4 per cent for 1979–80, the government's first year in office. There were two reasons for this. By the time the government was elected in May, public spending for the 1979–80 year was in full swing. It is difficult to cut down on public spending during the year (the analogy is with turning round a supertanker) and the cuts had to wait until 1980–81.

The other reason was that during the election campaign the Conservatives made certain pledges that required an initial rise in public spending, notably the decision to honour the recommendations of a special commission under Professor Hugh Clegg for large increases in public sector pay.

'The government is determined not merely to halt the growth of public spending but progressively to reduce it,' the 1980 White Paper said. Within this overall reduction, however, there were major differences in the targets for individual areas of public spending.

Planned increases and planned cuts
There were, firstly, those parts of public spending that the government wanted to increase quite sharply. Defence and law and order, both with double-figure percentage real increases over the four-year planning period, fell into this category, in line with pledges to boost spending on the police and the armed forces.

The second category of spending was where the government did not intend real cuts, but aimed to reduce growth sharply. It may come as a surprise to discover that the Conservatives did not intend cuts in the two most important areas of spending which fell into this category – the National Health Service and social security. It was the case for the social security budget, however, that the level of spending was planned to reach a plateau very quickly, and decline from that level.

The planned cuts in spending came in the third category and the list was a predictable one, including overseas aid, support for industry, lending to nationalized industries, education and the arts.

The cuts reflected the desire to increase private provision and reduce public provision. In the case of the arts, for example, private sponsorship was preferable to public subsidy. The housing budget would be sharply reduced, both by the sale of council houses to tenants and by a big reduction in the house-building programme.

Large-scale support and subsidy for industry had no place in Conservative free market philosophy. The Department of Industry's budget was cut. The nationalized industries were to be allowed to charge fair market prices for their services, with a corresponding reduction and eventual reversal of cash drain they imposed on central government.

Some of the planned cuts were very large indeed. The housing budget was to be virtually halved, and that for the Departments of Industry, Energy, Trade and Employment cut by over 40 per cent.

Cuts, what cuts?

The government's desire to cut public spending in real terms made itself felt in every office in every government department, and in schools, hospitals, university departments and other outposts of the public sector. Cuts there were. But the overall record of Mrs Thatcher's first four years was a large real increase in public spending, not a reduction.

Figure 4 tells the story. Had the government achieved its targets, both lines would have been gently declining from their 1979–80 peak. As we see, the lines are undoubtedly rising. The plans, if achieved, would have meant a real fall of over 4 per cent in public spending between 1979–80 and 1983–84. In fact, there was a rise of about 7.5 per cent, not much lower than the 10 per cent increase planned by the previous Labour government over a similar period.

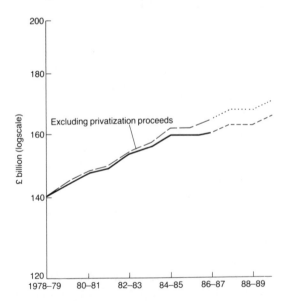

Figure 4 General government expenditure in real terms (public Expenditure White Paper, 1987, Part One)

What went wrong? If we run through our three categories very quickly, it is easy to see. For the favoured areas of spending – defence and law and order – providing the extra resources promised turned out to require a lot more public expenditure than planned. This was particularly the case for defence, where the annual rise in the price of defence equipment bought by the services far outstripped the general rate of inflation in the economy.

In the second category – the big demand-led areas of public spending, health and social security – the government made the mistake of badly under-estimating demand. The rising real cost of health care was one factor, but more important was the impact of sharply rising unemployment on the social security budget.

Unemployment rose from 1.2 million when the Conservatives were elected in 1979, to 3 million by the end of 1982. Each additional unemployed person added just under £2000 to public spending, through the payment of benefits (the actual loss to the government was greater because of the loss of income tax revenue as people became unemployed). Unemployment may also have added to the pressures on public spending in other areas. For example, if unemployment leads to more illness among the population, the demands on the National Health Service are increased.

In the third category, where real cuts in spending were planned, the government failed through being too ambitious and through not taking account of the sharp downturn in the economy that occurred, partly because of world recession, partly as a result of the policy of trying to squeeze inflation out of the system. The best example was lending to the nationalized industries. In spite of the declared intention of making state industries pay their way, the government – and in particular Mrs Thatcher's first Secretary of State for Industry, Sir Keith Joseph – faced a stream of demands from these industries for extra funds, demands brought on by a combination of recession and large public sector pay increases.

In many cases these extra funds had to be provided as part of a programme of providing redundancy payments as these industries cut down on the number of workers employed. There were well-publicized battles between the unions and management of British Leyland. A long and expensive strike at the British Steel Corporation in 1980 was eventually resolved in favour of the management. The same occurred in 1984–85 with the National Coal Board. Recession and rationalization produced a sharp increase in the financial demands emanating from the nationalized industries.

Phase two: Consolidation

The depth of Britain's recession was reached in the spring of 1981. The public expenditure planning process in Britain, the Public Expenditure Survey and Control (**PESC**) round, begins in the spring when ministers submit bids for the following year's spending to the Treasury. These bids are examined in detail in negotiations over the summer between departmental and Treasury officials. In September, battle commences between the Chief Secretary to the Treasury (the minister in the Treasury responsible for spending, second in command to the Chancellor of the Exchequer) and the spending ministers.

Any outstanding disputes between departments and the Treasury (and there are usually plenty) are resolved by the so-called **star chamber** of senior ministers. If the spending ministers do not accept the verdict, the Prime Minister is the final arbiter. In November, the Treasury publishes its autumn statement, containing spending targets for the financial year beginning the following April.

There is still scope for further spending adjustment between the autumn statement and the Budget, which is usually in March. The whole process lasts for about a year. Between the Budgets of March 1981 and March 1982, the government's overall goal for public spending shifted from one of trying to secure a steady real reduction, to that of holding it constant in real terms.

This was still a considerable ambition. The recession of 1979–81 had ensured strongly rising public expenditure. As Peter Riddell observed in his book (consult the reading list) on Mrs Thatcher's first term:

> 'Given the inherent upward pressures on expenditure on social security and the health service, the real question may be not why did public expenditure overshoot, but how did the government manage to contain the rise in the face of the deepest recession for fifty years? For example international figures compiled by the Organization for Economic Cooperation and Development show that public expenditure (after excluding transfer payments such as social security benefits) rose less in real terms in 1981 and 1982 in the UK than in any of the other big seven industrialized countries.'

The second phase of the public spending strategy, holding it constant in real terms, was no easy option. Although the emergence of the economy from recession eased the pressure on some of the demand-led areas of expenditure, the overall trend remained a rising one.

There were special factors such as the Falklands War, additional spending commitments ahead of the June 1983 election, and the 1984–85 miners' strike. But the overall message, which can be gleaned from Figure 4, is that public expenditure in Britain tends to rise by 1.5–2 per cent a year in real terms, come what may.

Phase three: Realism

This fact led to the third phase of the government's public spending strategy, that of allowing real increases but aiming to reduce the public expenditure share of GDP because the increases are smaller than those for the GDP. This was exemplified by the November 1986 autumn statement from the Treasury. It included big cash increases in spending: £4.7 billion in 1987–88 and £5.5 billion in 1988–89.

The extra spending was convenient in electoral terms, with a general election – won with a 100-seat majority by the Conservatives – held in June 1987. But it also reflected a new mood of realism on public spending – the official recognition that neither real cuts nor constant real spending could be achieved in practice. According to the Treasury:

> 'These plans mean that public spending is expected to fall as a proportion of the nation's income over the next three years. By 1989–90, the proportion is expected to be back to the levels of the early seventies. In real terms, public spending is expected to increase by an average of 1 per cent a year, significantly less than the growth of the nation's income.'

The test for this third phase of public spending policy will be whether this aim of securing a fall in public expenditure's share of national income is achieved, particularly when growth in the economy falters.

Current and capital spending

One persistent criticism of the government's record on public spending has been that, while **current spending** by the government (on benefits, public sector pay, etc.) has increased, **capital spending** (public investment in new roads, hospitals and the rest) has been cut back.

The Confederation of British Industry has complained that cutbacks in this area have deprived industry of orders, while producing a crumbling **infrastructure** – with roads, public buildings and sewers falling into disrepair. The argument is not an easy one to resolve. The Treasury says that the maintenance of the infrastructure falls within current spending and any reductions in the capital budget are irrelevant to this question. Current plans are for a real reduction in public sector capital spending of nearly 10 per cent over three years, but this figure is affected by the transfer of public corporations to the private sector (whereupon their investment becomes private investment).

Privatization

The government has shifted its ground on public expenditure, and the results of policy were not as first intended. With privatization, however, the results have exceeded the expectations even of the optimists in the Conservative party:

> 'Over a third of state-owned industry has been returned to free enterprise – 15 major businesses employing more than 600000 people. Free of state ownership and control, the profits of British Aerospace have trebled, those of Cable & Wireless are up four-fold, Amersham International's have doubled, Jaguar's are up a third and the National Freight Consortium's have increased seven-fold.
>
> 'Two million people bought British Telecom shares; five million bought shares in British Gas. Altogether the number of individual shareholders in Britain has trebled since 1979. One in five of the adult population is now a shareholder.' (1987 Conservative manifesto)

Privatization is the transfer of economic activity from the public to the private sector. It can be achieved by putting local authority refuse collection out to tender; or by allowing private bus companies to operate alongside state operators. But at its most dramatic it is the wholesale transfer of former nationalized industries into private ownership.

British Telecom used to be the telephones side of the Post Office. British Gas plc and Enterprise Oil were both part of the state-owned British Gas Corporation. Shares in British Petroleum and Cable & Wireless have been sold to eliminate the government's shareholding. The main airline in Britain, British Airways, has been sold off (as have the airports it and others use) through the flotation of the British Airports Authority. The National Freight Consortium is the largest employee buyout in the world. Britoil, Rolls-Royce, Associated British Ports, Amersham International, Jaguar and British Aerospace are all now quoted on the Stock Exchange as entirely private companies.

Privatization plays an important part in public finances. Sales of state assets count as **negative public spending**. As a result of privatization, the government currently has £5 billion a year more to use for spending or tax cuts than would otherwise be the case.

The sharp expansion of individual share ownership under the Conservatives would not have been possible without privatization. A survey published in 1987 by the Treasury and the Stock Exchange showed that share ownership increased from 7 per cent of the adult population in 1979 to nearly 20 per cent at the beginning of 1987, but that 8 per cent of the population held shares only in the privatized companies or the Trustee Savings Bank.

The government has instructed its financial advisers to market privatization issues heavily to the public. Attractive inducements to buy privatization shares, such as discount vouchers on gas and telephone bills, have been offered. The rationale is that the more people who own privatized shares, the greater will be the understanding of the need for profit in the economy, and the more difficult it will be for a future Labour government to take back privatized companies into public ownership.

Privatization, it is claimed, has sharply improved the performance of the former state industries, through the disciplines of the market. The government gains from the initial sale by raising money when such companies are floated. It also gains in the longer term, because these companies generate greater profits, part of which flow back to the government in the form of tax revenues.

The boards and managements of the former state corporations mostly prefer their new freedoms. They can raise money more easily on the capital markets, operate without having to refer to a sponsoring government department at every step, and pay themselves and their workers larger wage and salary increases.

Criticisms of privatization

There are plenty of criticisms of privatization, some of which can be summarized as follows:

- Privatization has simply transferred monopolies from the public to the private sector – it has produced no meaningful increase in competition.
- It has given people a distorted, 'casino' idea of share ownership, where instant gains can be made simply by subscribing to shares.
- The government has frittered away the proceeds of privatization in current public expenditure or tax cuts, rather than using them to improve the quality of the public sector capital stock – the infrastructure.
- The sale of the best parts of the public sector has left a rump of loss-making public corporations which will continue to be a drain on the Exchequer – their losses not offset by profits in other state-owned corporations.
- Privatization has deprived the government of the ability to use nationalized industries as a weapon of social policy – for example by creating employment in the depressed regions.

These criticisms do not alter the fact that it is with privatization rather than with the control of public expenditure that Mrs Thatcher's governments have been successful in reining back the public sector. And if the family silver has been sold, at least the new owners are keeping it well polished.

KEY WORDS

Public sector
Mixed economy
Crowding out
Public sector borrowing
    requirement
Gilts
Externalities
Privatization
Natural monopoly

IMF
Relative price effect
PESC
Star chamber
Current spending
Capital spending
Infrastructure
Negative public spending

Reading list

Bacon, Robert, and Eltis, Walter, *Britain's Economic Problem: Too Few Producers*, Macmillan, 1976.

Barnett, Joel, *Inside the Treasury*, André Deutsch, 1982.

Hurl, Bryan, *Privatization and the Public Sector*, Heinemann Educational Books, 1988.

Neuberger, Julia (ed.), *Privatisation – Fair Shares for All or Selling the Family Silver?*, Macmillan, 1987.

Pryke, Richard, *The Nationalised Industries*, Martin Robertson, 1981.

Riddell, Peter, *The Thatcher Government*, Martin Robertson, 1983.

Essay Topics

1. 'Public expenditure can never be controlled, governments can merely hope to slow the rate at which it increases.' Did Mrs Thatcher's government operate on this basis when it was elected in 1979? Does it now?
2. Some economists talk of 'crowding out'. What do they mean by this, and how would crowding out show itself?
3. 'A private sector monopoly is always better than a public sector monopoly.' Examine this statement with reference to the government's privatization of large public utilities such as British Gas and British Telecom.

4. What are externalities? How might society at large suffer if state industries are sold to the private sector, and what are the offsetting gains?

5. 'The government is determined not merely to halt the growth of public expenditure but progressively to reduce it' (1980 Public Expenditure White Paper). Did this determination translate into results, and why should governments set out to reduce public expenditure?

6. 'The real question may be not why did public expenditure overshoot, but how did the government manage to contain the rise in the face of the deepest recession for fifty years?' (Peter Riddell). Discuss.

7. Present the case for and against privatization.

8. 'Privatization is the only area where the government has successfully reined back the public sector.' Is this true?

Data Response Question 3
Public expenditure planning

Read the accompanying article from *The Times* of 8 November 1986.

1. What are the real increases in spending for 1986–87, 87–88 and 88–89?

2. Why were the plans described as a 'pre-election public spending boom'?

3. Why is the rate of growth of the economy important for the government's aim of reducing public expenditure's share of gross domestic product?

4. How has the Conservative government's record on public expenditure compared with that of the previous Labour government?

5. How does the sale of state assets (privatization) affect the public spending totals?

6. Would public spending growth under the Conservatives appear higher or lower if sales of assets were excluded?

7. Why are the spending plans characterized as a 'new realism'?

8. What do you understand by 'the £3.5 billion reserve'?

Real spending to rise by 2.1%

The full extent of the Chancellor's pre-election public spending boom was revealed yesterday by Treasury figures, showing that the bulk of the spending increase will take place in 1987–88, a fact not made clear by Mr Nigel Lawson's speech on Thursday.

The planning total for public spending

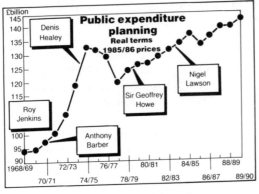

is targeted to rise by 2.1 per cent in real terms next year, after a 2.2 per cent rise in the present 1986–87 year. In the first financial year beyond the latest possible General Election date – 1988–89 – the rise is targeted to slow to only 0.2 per cent.

The figures emphasize that even a small undershoot in the Treasury's growth forecast would jeopardize the Government's aim of reducing the public sector's share of gross domestic product next year.

Treasury projections due out next week show that public spending's share of GDP will drop only slightly next year, from 43.25 per cent to 42.75 per cent.

The plans unveiled by the Chancellor show that the annual average growth in public spending since the Conservatives came to office will exceed that of the 1974–79 Labour Government.

In spite of efforts to control spending in the earlier years, real public spending under Mrs Thatcher will show average growth of 1.3 per cent a year, compared with an annual rate of 1 per cent under Mr Harold Wilson.

The figures show an even greater acceleration in public spending growth in the Thatcher years – in particular under Mr Lawson's Chancellorship – if allowance is made for sales of state assets.

The most significant difference between public spending control in the two periods appears to be that the Conservatives have pushed through spending cuts

while failing to exert control over public sector pay – and vice versa under Labour.

Although the Chancellor's statement was welcomed for containing a new realism on public spending, some observers and Treasury officials are unhappy about the new planning totals, because, based on past experience, they are likely to form the base, rather than the limit, for future departmental spending.

Next year's £3.5 billion reserve is not large by past standards and the Treasury appears to have assumed that pay settlements will be one percentage point lower than in the present year – an assumption questioned by many outside economists.

The autumn statement has been a chastening experience for some senior Treasury officials, not only because of the sudden shift in attitude from parsimony to generosity but also, say City economists, because the Treasury, in its forecast, has been leaned upon to produce the most favourable outcome for a likely election year.

The Treasury forecast extends only until the end of 1987.

David Smith
Economics Correspondent

Data Response Question 4
Public sector borrowing

Read the accompanying article from *The Times* of 19 November 1986.

1. Why is the PSBR 'the only remaining totem of the government's economic policy'?
2. Why is the PSBR difficult to predict?
3. What is the main reason why the PSBR is not a good measure of the fiscal deficit?
4. The public sector financial deficit is the PSBR adjusted for asset sales. Is it larger or smaller than the PSBR?
5. What has been happening to the public sector financial deficit since 1981–82?
6. What do you understand by the term 'cyclically adjusted financial deficit'?
7. Would you expect the deficit to be larger or smaller when the economy is growing strongly?
8. How did the PSBR once fit neatly into the framework of the government's economic policy?
9. Why does this framework no longer exist?
10. What is the main role of the PSBR in the present situation?

Veil of stringency over rise in Budget deficit

The public-sector borrowing requirement, which last month came in at just £9 million, has become the only remaining totem of the Government's economic policy.

Monetary targets have been all but abandoned, the public expenditure planning totals have become movable feasts, and, according to the evidence of Treasury officials to the Treasury and Civil Service Committee earlier this week, there is no target for the exchange rate, either formal or informal.

This leaves the PSBR as the anchor of economic policy. The Chancellor of the Exchequer, in a curiously Victorian phrase, has said the new spending plans unveiled in the autumn statement will result in "not a penny piece of additional borrowing".

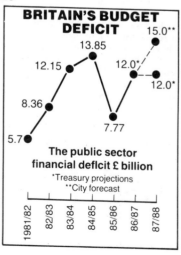

BRITAIN'S BUDGET DEFICIT

13.85
15.0**
12.15
12.0*
12.0*
8.36
7.77
5.7

The public sector financial deficit £ billion

*Treasury projections
**City forecast

1981/82 82/83 83/84 84/85 85/86 86/87 87/88

That is, of course, a meaningless statement. For one thing, it may be the spring tax cuts, rather than the autumn spending increases, which result in additional borrowing.

For another, the PSBR is difficult to predict and, as the Treasury has frequently reminded us, the PSBR is the difference between two very large numbers. And so nobody, not even Mr Lawson, can say with any certainty there will be no addition to borrowing next year.

Apart from the difficulty in forecasting it, the PSBR is not a good measure of the fiscal deficit. Distortions, some of them through the deliberate device of selling state assets, mean that the true budget deficit is some way away from the PSBR.

The public-sector financial deficit has been on an upward trend since 1981–82. This, strangely enough, was the point when the Government was supposed to have abandoned, for ever, the use of expansionary fiscal policies to boost the economy. In fact, it appeared to mark the point when, after a sharp contraction in the deficit, the Government decided that enough was enough.

The autumn statement contained an admitted expansion of the public sector deficit, by the device of adding to the targeted proceeds from asset sales.

A larger addition to the deficit is, however, expected when the final figures for the 1987–88 financial year become available, some time well after the next general election.

The public sector financial deficit has increased from a low point of less than £6 billion in 1981–82 to a coal-strike boosted £13.8 billion in 1984–85. This year, the deficit appears to have settled down to about £12 billion, although the City consensus is for a sharp rise in 1987–88, possibly to £15 billion.

These figures cast a very different light on the Government's apparent financial stringency. According to calculations by Goldman Sachs, the cyclically adjusted financial deficit, after contracting sharply in the period from 1979–80 to 1981–82, has been expansionary since then in every year apart from 1985–86.

The calculations show the Government applied a fiscal stimulus equivalent to 0.4 per cent of gross domestic product in 1982–83, 1.5 per cent in 1983–84 and 0.5 per cent in 1984–85. In 1985–86 there appears to have been a mis-calculation and an over-correction for the effects of the miners' strike, and there was a fiscal contraction equivalent to 1.6 per cent of GDP.

The economy, as Keynesians might have predicted, suffered from tighter fiscal policy, and the famous pause in economic growth, which began in the second quarter of 1985 and lasted until the first quarter of 1986, resulted.

Now, the Treasury has recognized that the hairshirt can be uncomfortable, and expansionary fiscal policy is once more the order of the day. Calculations, again from Goldman Sachs, suggest a fiscal stimulus equivalent to 1.1 per cent of GDP this year, followed by one of 0.7 per cent of GDP in 1987–88.

The public-sector borrowing requirement once fitted into the framework of the Government's economic policy fairly neatly, through the relationship between borrowing and broad money, sterling M3. Now, the main function of the PSBR is to appear as confirmation of the Government's financial rectitude. But this is not a job the PSBR does very well.

David Smith
Economics Correspondent

Chapter Four

Tax cuts and the supply side

'We shall cut income tax at all levels to reward hard work,
responsibility and success; tackle the poverty trap; encourage saving
and the wider ownership of property; simplify taxes – like VAT; and
reduce tax bureaucracy.

'It is especially important to cut the absurdly high marginal rates of
tax both at the bottom and top of the income scale. It must pay a man
or woman significantly more to be in, rather than out of, work.
Raising tax thresholds will let the low-paid out of the tax net
altogether, and unemployment and short-term sickness benefit must
be brought into the computation of annual income.

'The top rate of income tax should be cut to the European average
and the higher tax bands widened.' Conservative party manifesto,
1979

Direct and indirect taxation

Governments like to emphasize the taxes they plan to cut, and keep
quiet about those they are going to increase. The Conservative
manifesto held out the prospect of cuts in income tax – but an
important element of Conservative policy was not just reductions in
taxation but also a shift in the tax burden from direct to indirect
taxation.

Direct taxation, for individuals, consists of those taxes that are
levied directly on income. The main taxes in this category are therefore
income tax and national insurance contributions. Typically, income
tax is **progressive** in that the higher a person's income, the greater the
proportion of income taken in tax. This is achieved by having higher
marginal rates of income tax for higher income levels. (The **average
rate of income tax** is the amount you pay as a proportion of all
income, the **marginal rate** is the proportion taken in tax of each
individual pound of income.)

Unless they evade income tax (which is illegal) or employ financial
advisers to help avoid income tax (which is legal), people have to pay
it.

Indirect taxation for individuals consists of those taxes that are levied on spending. Value added tax (VAT) is the main one, together with the excise duties on, for example, alcohol, tobacco and petrol. Typically, such taxes are **regressive**, in that they are likely to take up a bigger proportion of a poor person's income than that of a rich person. A man earning £100 a week and smoking 20 cigarettes a day (leaving aside the question of whether he should be doing so) will pay the same amount of tax on his habit as a man earning £1000 a week and smoking the same amount. As a proportion of income, the poorer man is paying ten times as much.

There are ways of making indirect taxation less regressive – for example by setting higher rates of VAT on luxury goods such as caviar or silk shirts, or by setting zero rates of tax on basic necessities. In Britain, food and children's clothing are among the goods zero-rated for VAT purposes; but, unlike in some other EEC countries, there is no higher rate of VAT on luxuries.

The amount people pay in indirect taxation depends on what they spend. In an economy where all taxation was indirect, a rich person with basic needs would end up paying very little tax.

The 1979 budget

The first Budget of Mrs Thatcher's government, presented by Sir Geoffrey Howe on 12 June 1979, contained a substantial shift from direct to indirect taxation. This was partly because the new government thought such a change desirable; and it was partly because the cuts in income tax it wanted had to be largely financed elsewhere in the tax system, if public borrowing was to be kept under control.

Before the June 1979 Budget, top-rate taxpayers faced a marginal rate of income tax of 83 per cent on earned income and 98 per cent on earned and unearned (investment) income together. In the Budget these rates were reduced to 60 and 75 per cent respectively, implying a sharp reduction in taxation for the richest people in the population.

There was also a big cut in the standard or basic rate of income tax – the marginal rate faced by the majority of the population – from 33 to 30 per cent. There was therefore a general reduction in income tax to accompany the cut in the top rates.

The other side of the coin came with changes in VAT introduced at the same time. Before the Budget there had been a standard rate of VAT of 8 per cent, which applied to the majority of goods on which VAT was levied (goods like food and children's clothing were and still are zero-rated for VAT purposes). There was also a higher rate of 12.5

per cent for some 'luxury' products. In the Budget these rates were increased to a uniform VAT rate of 15 per cent.

At Budget time, the Treasury provides estimates of the revenue effects of tax changes both for the forthcoming financial year (or in this case the financial year already in progress, 1979–80) and for a full year. The latter are the effects calculated on the basis that the new tax rates are in force for a whole year and are free of distortions such as spending ahead of VAT increases. The 1979 income tax reductions were calculated to have a full-year revenue cost of £4.5 billion. This was almost exactly offset by the VAT changes, which were reckoned to bring in an extra £4.2 billion.

Within these tax changes which were, in overall terms, broadly **revenue-neutral**, there were important effects on the **distribution of income**. I noted earlier that indirect taxes are regressive: so with the extra VAT, paid by everyone from pensioners to millionaires, the extra burden on the pensioner, as a proportion of income, was much greater than that for the millionaire.

Taken in tandem with the fact that the biggest cuts in income tax were for the richest members of the population, this makes it clear that the effect of the June 1979 Budget was to shift the distribution of (post-tax) income in favour of the rich and away from the poor.

Why cut income tax?

The 1979 Budget was the only example under Mrs Thatcher of a substantial shift from direct to indirect taxation. The later emphasis was on cutting income tax, either through reductions in the basic rate of tax, or through raising the allowances and thresholds at which people begin to pay tax at different rates. In fact, as we shall see later, the overall tax burden faced by most people did not come down.

But why cut income tax? Apart from the political reason that if you give people tax handouts they are more likely to vote for you again (although opinion poll evidence has suggested a high level of cynicism among the British population about tax cuts), there are economic arguments for lowering income tax. They can be summarized as follows:

- Lower rates of income tax enhance incentives by allowing people to keep a greater proportion of the income they earn. People will work harder, spurred on by the knowledge that the extra money they earn is mainly for themselves, and not for the taxman.
- Income tax reductions – and in particular cuts in the higher rates of tax – create an atmosphere in which enterprise flourishes. People

will not bother to take the risk of setting up in business if they know that, even if successful, they will just end up paying more and more tax. Lower tax rates change all this.

- The lower the income tax rates, the less is the incentive for people to evade or avoid taxation. The unofficial 'black economy' – the cash economy that goes on beyond the taxman's eye – has less reason to exist. People are less likely to take the risk of getting caught evading tax if the tax they would have to pay in the first instance seemed reasonable.
- The process of cutting income tax may have a beneficial effect on the rate at which pay is rising in the economy. Union representatives, knowing that their members are to receive a 'bonus' from tax cuts, may be less likely to push for big wage increases.
- Reductions in income tax, if properly implemented, can alleviate the poverty trap. The poverty trap exists for people on very low incomes. Their income is made up of earnings from work and from social security benefits. If their earnings increase, the social security benefits they receive are gradually withdrawn, because they are related to income. The situation can exist where a person on a low income simultaneously loses benefits and starts to pay income tax, with the consequence that the effective marginal rate of tax is very high, in some cases above 100 per cent.
- A related problem where income tax reductions could help is with the unemployment trap. A person who is unemployed and receiving benefits may find that after taking a job their net income actually falls, because income tax has to be paid on earnings. This problem is often characterized as the 'Why work?' syndrome.

Tax cuts and incentives

What determines how long or how hard people work? Economists usually start to answer this question by defining a trade-off, for individuals, between work and leisure. In such a model, work is unpleasant while leisure is pleasant. There is a trade-off between the two, work being necessary to pay for the enjoyment of leisure.

This trade-off can be expressed, as in Figure 5, in the form of an indifference curve. The individual is indifferent between high income and a small number of leisure hours, the opposite situation of low income and plenty of leisure, and points in between. Another line in Figure 5, budget line 1, relates hours of leisure to income – the greater the time spent in leisure, the smaller the income. The optimum point is

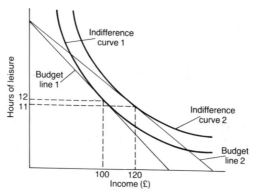

Figure 5 Indifference curves

reached when the indifference curve just touches the budget line, and this is the point at which the individual would choose to operate. He has a post-tax weekly income of £100 and enjoys 12 hours of leisure.

Now let us consider the effects of a cut in income tax. Our individual has worked out that, in order to pay for his leisure, he needs a certain fixed amount of post-tax income. A reduction in income tax increases post-tax income. The individual can afford to work fewer hours for the same take-home pay. This is a disincentive effect of lower taxation, and is known as the **income effect** of the tax change.

Furthermore there is another effect, the so-called **substitution effect**. A reduction in income tax means that leisure has become, in terms of income foregone, more expensive. The **opportunity cost** of leisure has increased because the post-tax income from each additional hour worked has risen. The substitution effect pulls in the opposite direction to the income effect – it provides an incentive to work longer hours.

In practice both income and substitution effects will appear, and the results of a cut in income tax are difficult to predict. In Figure 5 the effect of a tax cut is to produce a shift in the budget line to line 2 and a move to a new indifference curve (curve 2) outside the existing one. But the exact effect on the work/leisure trade-off will depend on the extent to which the tax cut has changed the *slope* of the budget line.

In our example, the effect of the tax cut is to increase the number of hours worked. The new intersection is at a daily number of 11 hours of leisure and a higher post-tax weekly income of £120.

Incentive effects in practice

The debate over the incentive effects of tax cuts has been a fierce one. Some economists say that tax cuts make no difference to how hard or how long people work. Others say that incentive effects are very strong indeed.

A study commissioned by the Treasury, and carried out by a research team under Professor C.V. Brown of the University of Stirling, was published in 1987. It concluded, embarrassingly for the government, that cuts in income tax did not make people work longer hours, suggesting very weak incentive effects. Most employees, the study said, could not work any longer hours in their main job even if they wanted to. Some 79 per cent of employees were said to be restricted in this way.

On the other hand, Professor P. Minford of the University of Liverpool, one of the leading lights of **supply-side economics** in Britain, says that cuts in tax rates motivate people to work and earn more to the extent that, following a cut in tax rates, tax revenues actually rise rather than fall.

A middle ground has been provided by the independent Institute for Fiscal Studies. It takes sides with the Brown study in that, in its view, only very large cuts in income tax would make any difference to the working behaviour of what has traditionally been regarded as the backbone of the workforce – prime-age married men. But the IFS believes – and its tax models support this view – that cuts in tax rates are important in encouraging married women to take jobs, or to work longer hours in existing jobs.

And certainly, between 1983 and 1987, much of the one million-plus growth in employment in Britain was in part-time jobs for women.

The Laffer curve

I referred above to Professor Minford's argument that lower tax rates, by boosting incentive, produce a net gain in tax revenues. This view was embodied in the **Laffer curve**, drawn up by the American supply-side economist Professor A. Laffer.

The Laffer curve is simple (see Figure 6). It starts by saying that there are two points – when the average tax rate is zero and when it is 100 per cent – when the government will receive no tax revenues. In the first case it is because no tax is levied. In the second it is because, if the average tax rate is 100 per cent, people are doing all their work for the taxman and it is not worth working.

Between these two points, Laffer suggested, tax revenues will move in such a way that there comes a point when higher tax rates reduce tax revenues, because it is not worth working as much. And, looking

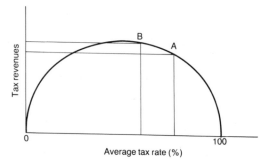

Figure 6 The Laffer curve

at this the other way around, we can see the supply-side case for lowering tax rates.

Starting from position A in Figure 6, where tax rates are high, a reduction in rates could push us to position B, with lower rates but higher revenues. The government is then happy because it has gained both revenue and popularity. Individuals are happy because they face lower tax rates.

The Laffer curve has been strongly criticized. Indeed, even its creator has been reluctant to push it as a fully fledged theory. Critics say that even if one accepts Laffer's starting points, there is no evidence that the curve between those points runs in the way he suggested. There is also the criticism that Laffer's analysis is in terms of average tax rates and tells us little that is useful about marginal rates – and marginal rates are the ones that governments have to make decisions on.

Supply-side evidence

After cutting the basic rate of income tax from 29 to 27 per cent in his March 1987 Budget, the Chancellor of the Exchequer said: 'Lower rates of tax sharpen up incentives and stimulate enterprise, which in turn is the only route to better economic performance.'

In the testing ground of Mrs Thatcher's economic policies, there are two areas where, it is argued, this claim stands up. The first is the experience since 1979 for higher-rate taxpayers. In 1978–79, 24 per cent of income tax revenue was paid by the top 5 per cent of income earners. By 1985–86, in spite of the large 1979 cut in the higher rates of income tax, this proportion had risen to 26.7 per cent. Therefore, it is claimed, incentive effects have clearly worked. Enterprise, a proxy for which could be the increase in the number of higher-rate tax-payers, has flourished.

47

This argument is by no means clear-cut. It is challenged by economists who argue that the government's policies have produced a sharp shift in the distribution of income in favour of the rich, which has had little to do with enterprise. So a greater proportion of tax paid by the top 5 per cent may simply reflect greater *income inequality*, arising from very big income increases for the rich.

The second test case is not for individuals but for companies. In his 1984 Budget the Chancellor announced a *phased reduction* in the rate of **corporation tax** from 52 to 35 per cent. Alongside this, however, he announced the withdrawal of certain tax reliefs.

In the high-inflation 1970s, measures had been introduced to allow companies to offset against tax the rise in the value of their stocks which resulted simply from inflation. This stock appreciation relief was abolished 'in 1984. In addition, companies had been entitled to set outlays on capital equipment against tax, in order to encourage investment: up to 100 per cent of capital expenditure could be claimed against corporation tax in this way. The 1984 Budget announced the *phased abolition* of these capital allowances.

After the tax changes, which featured lower corporation tax rates, there was an increase in corporation tax revenues. In the 1986–87 financial year, a large rise in these revenues was partly responsible for the fact that the public sector borrowing requirement came in at half the Treasury's £7 billion target. Was this an example of companies striving harder to make profits because tax rates were reduced?

Again, the argument is not clear-cut. The Institute for Fiscal Studies said when the changes were introduced that the net effect of lower tax rates and the removal of tax reliefs was to increase companies' tax liabilities. The fact that the changes were followed by a period when, because of general conditions in the economy, company profits were in any case strong, means that the reduction in corporation tax rates cannot be held up as the only reason – or even the main reason – for higher corporation tax revenues.

The black economy

Where there is taxation there is also usually a black economy. The black economy (also known as the cash, hidden, shadow or underground economy) consists of activities carried out without officialdom – and in particular the taxman – knowing about them. Everyone knows of the tradesman who insists on cash-only payments, or the businessman who apparently gets everything paid for by his company, including his car, house and clothing.

Estimates of the size of the black economy vary. In Italy it is said to be the equivalent of one-third of the size of the officially recorded economy. In Britain, estimates range from about 3 per cent of national income up to 15 or 20 per cent. Sir William Pile, when chairman of the Inland Revenue, said that the black economy was equivalent to 7.5 per cent of national income. By its nature, no-one can tell the size of the black economy with any certainty.

If the black economy is regarded as a bad thing (and Sir Geoffrey Howe, Mrs Thatcher's first Chancellor, said that untaxed perks – one aspect of the black economy – were wasteful and divisive), then there are, broadly, two ways of reducing its size.

The first is to tighten up policing arrangements by increasing the number of tax inspectors, and to make penalties more severe. This has been done to an extent. Small businessmen complain of the attentions they receive from VAT inspectors. Income tax inspectors have become more vigilant when dealing with those occupations where the black economy is known to thrive.

The other route to killing off the black economy is to reduce taxation to levels at which it is not worth taking the risk of being caught evading tax, so more people opt for earning and paying tax legally.

The black economy is undoubtedly unfair in that the tax burden is unevenly shared. Some would say, however, that without the black economy things would operate less efficiently. (Anyone seeking to have building work done on a private house in the prosperous South East of England, for example, might find that they had to wait a very long time indeed if the black economy was entirely eliminated.) And it is doubtful whether tax cuts in themselves have much impact on the black economy: the taxation of perks such as company cars has made these less attractive than they were. Reductions in income tax are unlikely to make people switch in large numbers to the official economy.

The government set itself a target of reducing the basic rate of income tax to 25 per cent – a target achieved in the March 1988 Budget. That is still quite a high rate for someone who is of a mind to evade paying tax altogether. What is more, anyone declaring taxable income for the first time might have some difficulty explaining to the taxman about undeclared income in previous years.

The poverty trap

Consider the case of a low-paid family man who earns £100 a week in his job, which is roughly half of average national earnings. In addition to this he receives £50 in social security benefits, because of the needs of his family.

Now suppose that his employer gives him a £20 a week pay increase. Will he be £20 a week better off? Probably not. The Department of Health and Social Security will withdraw £20 of his £50 a week benefits, leaving him trapped on a weekly income of £150.

The position could be even worse than that. A man in his circumstances might be below the threshold at which income tax has to be paid on his original income of £100 a week, but the rise to £120 could put him in the position of having to pay tax. If he has to pay £5 a week in tax then the situation could arise whereby, as a result of the £20 a week increase, he ends up with an income from all sources of just £145. His effective marginal rate of tax — because of the simultaneous withdrawal of benefits and a move into tax-paying — is *more* than 100 per cent. A pay increase of £20 has left him £5 a week worse off.

A reduction in tax rates would not help this family's plight very much; but an increase in the point at which the man starts to pay tax — by raising allowances and thresholds — could help to alleviate the problem. This was the method by which the government attempted to reduce the tax burden between 1980 and 1985.

Another development that has helped alleviate the worst features of the poverty trap has been to make all income — both taxes and benefits — subject to tax. The 1988 reforms of social security, with the new family income support, will also help get rid of the very high marginal rates of taxation/benefit withdrawal for those on low incomes.

The fact remains that, for many people on low incomes, only very large increases in earnings would allow them to break out of the poverty trap.

The unemployment trap

A close relative of the poverty trap is the unemployment trap. Returning to the example above, consider the situation in which our family man, instead of obtaining part of his income from work and part from the Department of Health and Social Security, receives the entire £150 a week in the form of benefits. He is offered a job at £100 a week which, with the parallel withdrawal of some benefits, would leave his income unchanged at £150 a week. There is no *monetary* incentive for him to take this low-paid job, so he is trapped in unemployment.

Professor Minford of the University of Liverpool has calculated that an unskilled family man would need to be paid £180 a week or more before it became worth while for him to take up employment.

There are two ways of tackling this problem. The 'stick' of threatening the removal of benefits if people do not take up work that is offered can be used instead of the 'carrot' of incentives for taking up a job.

Another suggestion has been the complete recasting of the income tax structure to include a **negative rate of income tax**. Under such a system, low-paid people would be on a negative rate of income tax – they would receive a payout from the government. As they moved up the income scale, this negative rate would decline until they reached the point at which they were paying normal, positive rates of income tax. Such a system, implying the integration of the tax and benefit systems, could ensure that incentives were part of the framework; but it still might not create much incentive to take up very low-paid jobs.

The threat of withdrawal of benefits – which the government intends to apply to young people who do not take up employment or a Youth Training Scheme place – may sound draconian; but it *was* envisaged in the Beveridge Report as long ago as 1944. Sweden, which has successfully pursued a full employment policy through the difficulties of the 1970s and 1980s, applies such rules.

Tax cuts and wages

The Conservative government has emphasized the growth in real wages as one factor contributing to high unemployment. Slower growth in wages (or even real wage reductions) would, it has been argued, reduce unemployment. This runs counter to the traditional Keynesian argument whereby reducing wages cuts demand in the economy and results in higher unemployment.

The difficulty has been – with incomes policies having no place in the government's philosophy, and with such policies of questionable long-term effectiveness – how *do* you slow the growth in wages?

One suggestion is that income tax cuts, by automatically increasing take-home pay, may act as a dampener on excessive pay rises. A study in the National Institute *Economic Review* as long ago as 1976 found that tax cuts were the most effective weapon for governments wishing to reduce the rate of growth of wages. Other studies have found that the level of the **retention ratio** (the proportion of income that the employee takes home after tax) does not make much difference to pay rises. Therefore, the case seems to be made for a stream of tax reductions, each of which has an impact on a pay round.

The evidence during Mrs Thatcher's years in office for a slowdown in wages brought on by reductions in income tax rates is very thin. The tax cuts of the June 1979 Budget were followed by a sharp increase in wages, partly because cuts in income tax rates had been accompanied by higher VAT and a general upturn in inflation. The tax cuts of 1986 and 1987 had no noticeable impact on pay settlements.

In any case, the use of tax cuts in this way could only be a short-term palliative. Governments cannot, in practice, hope to cut taxes indefinitely. The solution to pay problems has to lie within the wage bargaining process itself.

The Thatcher record on tax cuts

In the nine Budgets from 1979 to 1987, Mrs Thatcher's governments cut income tax in all except one. The exception was the austerity Budget of 1981.

In 1979, 1986, 1987 and 1988 there were cuts in income tax rates. In 1979 the top rate of income tax on earnings was reduced from 83 to 60 per cent and the basic rate from 33 to 30 per cent. In 1986 the basic rate was cut to 29 per cent, in 1987 to 27 per cent and in 1988 to 25

Table 2 Treasury figures for persons on 50 per cent of male average earnings (£113.65 in 1987–88)

	Single		Married with 2 children	
	£ per week	Per cent of gross income	£ per week	Per cent of gross income
1978–79				
Income tax	7.91	17.0	3.26	6.3
National Insurance	3.02	6.5	3.02	5.9
Totals	10.93	23.6	6.28	12.2
1983–84				
Income tax	15.35	18.0	9.53	9.8
National Insurance	7.70	9.0	7.70	7.9
Totals	23.05	27.0	17.23	17.6
1987–88				
Income tax	18.09	15.9	10.98	8.6
National Insurance	10.23	9.0	10.23	8.0
Totals	28.32	24.9	21.21	16.6

Table 3 Treasury figures for persons on male average earnings (£227.30 a week in 1987–88)

| | Single | | Married with 2 children | |
	£ per week	Per cent of gross income	£ per week	Per cent of gross income
1978–79				
Income tax	23.22	25.0	18.46	18.8
National Insurance	6.03	6.5	6.03	6.2
Totals	29.25	31.5	24.49	25.0
1983–84				
Income tax	41.00	24.6	35.18	19.2
National Insurance	15.39	9.0	15.39	8.4
Totals	46.39	33.6	50.57	27.6
1987–88				
Income tax	48.78	21.5	41.67	17.2
National Insurance	20.46	9.0	20.46	8.5
Totals	69.24	30.5	62.13	25.7

per cent. The government has set a target of reducing the basic rate to 20 per cent and in March 1988 reduced the top rate to 40 per cent.

In 1980, 1982, 1983, 1984 and 1985, as well as in some of the other years alongside rate cuts, tax allowances and thresholds were raised by more than inflation. This 'over-indexing' of allowances is simply another way of cutting tax, by moving the point at which people start paying tax. It was favoured as a way of taking people out of tax in the first half of the 1980s, partly because of its greater effect on the poverty and unemployment traps.

Income tax is not, however, the only direct tax that people pay. National Insurance contributions are also levied directly on income, and in some years these were increased at the same time as income tax was cut.

In his 1984 Budget the Chancellor of the Exchequer introduced measures to ease the burden of National Insurance on the lower paid, involving reduced rates for those on low earnings. Clearly, National Insurance has to be taken into account in assessing the government's tax-cutting record.

Tables 2–4 examine the tax positions of various income groups.

Three different points have been selected: immediately before the Conservative government took office (1978–79), roughly halfway through (1983–84), and the latest position as this analysis was being written (1987–88). You should examine these tables because they will form the basis of a data response question at the end of this chapter.

The tables give us the facts of changes in direct taxation under Mrs Thatcher. For the low paid (Table 2 shows those on 50 per cent of average earnings) the proportion of income taken by income tax and National Insurance contributions was higher in 1987–88 than in 1978–79. For these people there has been no reduction in the tax burden.

For those on average earnings (Table 3) the record for the first four years was poor, with the proportion of income taken in income tax and National Insurance contributions rising. Since then it has come down, but the direct tax burden for the 'typical' man on average earnings with two children was still slightly higher in 1987–88 than in 1978–79.

Table 4 Treasury figures for persons on five times male average earnings (£1136.50 a week in 1987–88)

	Single		Married with 2 children	
	£ per week	Per cent of gross income	£ per week	Per cent of gross income
1978–79				
Income tax	234.37	50.5	223.55	47.7
National Insurance	7.80	1.7	7.80	1.7
Totals	242.17	52.2	231.35	49.3
1983–84				
Income tax	364.42	42.6	352.77	40.7
National Insurance	21.15	2.5	21.15	2.4
Totals	385.57	45.1	373.92	43.1
1987–88				
Income tax	493.50	43.4	477.69	41.5
National Insurance	26.55	2.3	26.55	2.3
Totals	520.05	45.8	504.24	43.8

For the top earners (Table 4) the Conservatives' first Budget provided a major boost. People in this category now pay a substantially smaller proportion of income in direct taxation than when Mrs Thatcher took office. The main effect was early in the lifetime of her government. It will be noted that since 1983–84 there has been a small rise in the tax burden on the well-off, but this will be reversed by the impact of the 1988 Budget.

National Insurance, which is a very important factor in these calculations, is deducted from income at source for employees (not for the self-employed). As with income tax, the more you earn the more, in general, you pay. However, there is a cut-off point for National Insurance above which contributions for employees do not increase. The upper earnings limit in 1987–88 was £280 a week. Thus, someone earning £600 or £1000 a week paid the same in National Insurance as a person on £280 a week.

The logic for this approach is that National Insurance payments are, as their name suggests, contributions to the National Insurance Fund. If one takes the insurance analogy as appropriate, there is no reason why premiums should rise indefinitely with income. In practical terms, on the other hand, setting a limit for National Insurance contributions makes the tax system more regressive than it would otherwise be.

The general tax picture

I have so far discussed the government's record on direct taxation. What about the wider picture, taking in all forms of taxation? Have we become more or less taxed under Mrs Thatcher?

For the country as a whole the tax burden has undoubtedly increased. Comparative figures from the Organization for Economic Cooperation and Development show Britain to be roughly in the middle of the international league table on tax. But, as in most other countries, the overall tax burden has risen in recent years. Total taxation has risen from the equivalent of around 32 per cent of gross domestic product when Mrs Thatcher came to power in 1979, to 39 per cent in 1986.

Treasury figures show a rise in overall taxation levels for most individuals, as Table 3 based on average earnings shows.

The government has set a target of reducing income tax further, taking the basic rate to 20 per cent. The evidence is that sizeable tax reductions are still needed to return to the tax position that Mrs Thatcher inherited.

KEY WORDS

Direct taxation	Unemployment trap
Progressive	Indifference curve
Average rate of income tax	Income effect
Marginal rate	Substitution effect
Indirect taxation	Opportunity cost
Regressive	Supply-side economics
Revenue-neutral	Laffer curve
Distribution of income	Corporation tax
Black economy	Negative rate of income tax
Poverty trap	Retention ratio

Reading list

Bartlett, Bruce, 'Supply-side economics: theory and evidence', *National Westminster Quarterly Review*, February 1985.

Kay, J.A., and King, M.A., *The British Tax System*, Oxford University Press, 1983.

Lomax, D.F., 'Supply-side economics: the British experience', *National Westminster Quarterly Review*, August 1982.

Owens, Jeffrey, 'Tax reform: an international perspective', *National Westminster Quarterly Review*, May 1987.

Smith, Stephen, *Britain's Shadow Economy*, Oxford University Press, 1986.

Essay Topics

1. 'A regressive tax system is necessary to encourage enterprise.' Discuss, drawing out the difference between progressive and regressive taxation.
2. Examine the case for lower rates of income tax. Have tax cuts had beneficial effects in Britain since 1979?
3. Describe the income and substitution effects of a reduction in direct taxation. Will most people work harder if their tax rates are reduced?
4. 'The black economy would exist even at very low rates of tax.' Discuss, defining the black economy and describing its relationship with rates of taxation.
5. The poverty and unemployment traps affect people on low incomes. Describe how they work and discuss whether changes in taxation or in social security benefits are more likely to alleviate them.

6. 'Lower rates of tax sharpen up incentives and stimulate enterprise, which in turn is the only route to better economic performance' (Nigel Lawson). Describe the incentive effects of lower tax rates, with reference to the British economy since 1979.
7. What is the case for shifting the burden of taxation from direct taxes such as income tax, to indirect taxes such as VAT? What problems were encountered when this policy was pursued in 1979?
8. The tax burden has risen from 32 to 39 per cent under Mrs Thatcher. (a) Define the tax burden in this context. (b) Examine the reasons for its rise. (c) Discuss whether an overall rise in the tax burden means that everyone is paying a greater proportion of their income in tax.

Data Response Question 5
Some specific tax examples

Study Table 5, and refer back to Tables 2–4. Then answer the following questions.

1. In the three financial years covered, when was the highest proportion of direct taxation (income tax plus National Insurance)) paid by a single person on 50 per cent of male average earnings?
2. What was that proportion?
3. When was the corresponding peak reached for a single person on five times average earnings, and what was that proportion?
4. On the basis of the evidence in Tables 2–4 would you say that National Insurance is a progressive or a regressive tax?
5. Examine, in each earnings group in Tables 2–4, the proportion of tax paid by single people and those who are married with two children. Comparing 1978–79 and 1987–88, have the tax advantages of marrying and having children become more or less?
6. In terms of the amount of tax paid, a single person on five times average earnings paid more than five times the amount of a person on average earnings in 1987–88. What is the explanation for this?
7. For a single person on average earnings, the proportion of income paid in income tax has fallen quite sharply between 1978–79 and 1987–88. Why, then, has there been only a small proportional decrease in the direct tax burden?
8. In 1987–88, how much more, in money terms, would a person on 50 per cent of average earnings pay in direct taxation if he obtained a job which paid average earnings?

Table 5 Treasury figures for taxes paid to central and local government by persons on average earnings

	Single		Married with 2 children	
	£ per week	Per cent of gross income	£ per week	Per cent of gross income
1978–79				
Income tax	23.22	25.0	18.46	18.8
National Insurance	6.03	6.5	6.03	6.2
VAT	2.46	2.7	2.43	2.5
Other indirect taxes	7.54	8.1	7.91	8.1
Domestic rates	2.87	3.1	2.79	2.8
Totals	42.12	45.4	37.61	38.4
1987–88				
Income tax	48.78	21.5	41.67	17.2
National Insurance	20.46	9.0	20.46	8.5
VAT	10.94	4.8	11.24	4.6
Other indirect taxes	17.31	7.6	18.13	7.5
Domestic rates	8.56	3.8	8.20	3.4
Totals	106.04	46.7	99.70	41.2

9. Referring to Table 5 which categories of taxation have risen, as a proportion of income, for a person on average earnings between 1978–79 and 1987–88?
10. Give some examples of 'other indirect taxes'.
11. In Table 5, has the overall tax burden risen more for single people or for those who are married with two children?
12. For a single person on average earnings, how much, in money terms, would total tax paid need to be in 1987–88 for the tax burden to have remained unchanged on its 1978–79 level?

Data Response Question 6
International tax comparisons

Read the accompanying article from *The Times* of 18 July 1986.

1. Does the OECD evidence suggest that the government has been successful in reducing the tax burden?

2. Relative to the OECD average, has the tax burden in Britain moved higher or lower?
3. What is the distinction between direct and indirect taxation?
4. What are the figures for direct taxation (including National Insurance) and indirect taxation as a proportion of total tax revenues in Britain?
5. How does the proportion of taxation raised in Britain by indirect taxes compare with other countries?
6. Does the government need to increase this proportion to move into line with other countries?
7. What has happened to the tax burden for the OECD countries, and for Britain, over a 20-year period?
8. Which country has been the recent exception to the general trend of rising taxation, and why?

UK taxes 'on a par with average of Western world'

RELATIVE TAX BURDENS
(as % of gross domestic product)

	1980	1981	1982	1983	1984	1985
Sweden	49.36	51.05	49.92	50.59	50.46	50.60
Denmark	45.48	45.34	44.48	46.47	48.02	49.40
Norway	47.10	48.67	47.92	46.66	46.41	47.80
Netherlands	45.82	45.19	45.43	47.03	45.54	44.78
France	42.53	42.80	43.79	44.57	45.49	45.55
Italy	33.21	36.14	38.91	42.10	41.17	n/a
Ireland	34.04	35.27	37.03	38.70	39.48	38.37
United Kingdom	35.33	36.51	39.27	37.91	38.51	38.58
Germany	38.00	37.57	37.44	37.45	37.73	37.97
Canada	32.05	34.07	33.74	33.37	33.72	34.18
Switzerland	30.78	30.56	31.00	31.58	32.18	32.04
United States	30.35	30.77	30.55	29.03	28.99	n/a
Japan	25.45	26.24	26.66	27.20	27.38	n/a
OECD average	**35.26**	**36.21**	**36.56**	**36.94**	**37.11**	**n/a**

Source OECD: ranked by 1984 figures

Britain is not a high tax country, according to the latest comparative figures from the Organization for Economic Co-operation and Development in Paris.

In the annual league table drawn up by the OECD, Britain occupies a middle position, with tax revenues accounting for just above 38 per cent of national income.

Britain's figure is well below the Scandinavian countries, all with tax revenues of close to 50 per cent of national income. It is roughly the same as West Germany, but well above Japan and the US.

The average for the Western industrialized countries which make up the OECD is for total taxation of around 37 per cent of national income.

The OECD's *Revenue Statistics* also show what types of taxation are used. In a comparison of tax receipts in 1984, the report shows that in Britain 38.2 per cent of taxation is on income and company profits, although to this can be added the other direct form of personal taxation, national insurance, which accounts for a further 18.1 per cent.

Indirect taxation – value-added tax and excise duties – provided 30.5 per cent of total tax receipts, while the remaining 12.2 per cent came from property taxes.

The figures suggest that the balance between direct taxation, those on income and profits, and indirect, those on spending, is not badly wrong in Britain. It has been an aim of this Government to tilt the burden in favour of more indirect taxation.

In the US, income, profits and social security taxes accounted for 71.5 per cent of federal revenues, compared with 18.2 per cent for taxes on goods and services. The comparison is, however, complicated by the incidence of state indirect taxation.

Even so, in Japan only 15 per cent of tax revenues are from the spending taxes, while in West Germany the figure is 27 per cent.

In several countries, including the Scandinavian countries and Spain, direct taxation accounts for about 70 per cent of total revenues.

Twenty years ago, in the OECD countries, tax revenues were equivalent to about 27 per cent of national income. Ten years later, the figure had increased to 33 per cent. The lastest complete figure, for 1984, is more than 37 per cent.

In Britain, the latest estimate of the tax burden, 38.58 per cent of national income last year, is an increase on the two previous years, but is not the highest level ever. In 1982, tax revenues were equivalent to 39.27 per cent.

In the mid-1960s, tax revenues were equal to just above 30 per cent.

The US is the only important economy to have achieved a reversal in the rising taxation trend. Its tax as a proportion of national income has fallen continuously over the past three years as a result of President Reagan's tax cuts. The ratio of tax to national income, 28.99 per cent in 1984, is only 2.7 percentage points higher than its level 20 years earlier.

David Smith
Economics Correspondent

Chapter Five

Union law and the labour market

'*A fair balance between the rights and obligations of unions, management and the community in which they work is essential to economic recovery. They should provide the stable conditions in which pay bargaining can take place as responsibility in Britain as it does in other countries.*

'*Free trade unions can only flourish in a free society. A strong and responsible trade union movement could play a big part in our economic recovery. We cannot go on, year after year, tearing ourselves apart in increasingly bitter and calamitous industrial disputes. In bringing about economic recovery, we should all be on the same side.*' Conservative party manifesto, 1979

The role of the unions

Mass trade unionism developed in Britain in the second half of the nineteenth century. Unions were illegal until 1824 and grew only slowly, largely in craft occupations – skilled trades such as cutlery and furniture making – in the following 50 years. In 1870, well into Britain's industrial development, there were only about 500 000 union members.

From the end of the 1880s until the outbreak of the First World War in 1914, trade union membership grew rapidly, rising to about eight million. The chief cause was the spreading of unionization into non-craft occupations, and into the mass-employment industries such as road, rail and water transport and the iron and steel industries.

After the First World War the growth of the trade unions paralleled the emergence and growth of the Labour party. The General Strike of 1926 was a failure, but it was also a reminder of the potential force of organized labour.

For most of the twentieth century the trade unions have played a key role in the politics and economics of Britain, a role which has gone beyond that of simply representing their members in bargaining over pay and conditions.

The image of trade union leaders being invited to 10 Downing Street for beer and sandwiches has become a cliché; but it is indicative of a time, in the 1960s and 70s, when governments could hardly make a move without the agreement of the powerful trade unions.

All this has changed. If Mrs Thatcher's aim was to reduce the power of the unions, then she and her governments have certainly succeeded. In terms of power, influence and membership, the unions are but a shadow of their former selves. The role of the National Economic Development Council, which brought together the government, industry and the unions, has been scaled down. **Corporatism** – decision-making arrived at jointly by the powerful unions, the most influential industrialists and the government – is dead.

The interesting question is whether this has come about as a result of union reform or because of general economic conditions since 1979. I shall examine this a little later, but first let us look at some of the theory about trade unions and their effects.

Unions and pay

Figure 7 is a representation of the supply and demand for labour in an industry. We begin from a position where the industry is non-unionized. The supply of labour in this situation is represented by the line S_1. In the absence of unions, each worker is competing against all others. No one individual can threaten to withdraw his labour or someone else will take his job. There are no entry restrictions preventing people from working in the industry. There are, therefore, a large number of people willing to work at most wage rates. Higher wages do produce an increase in the supply of labour – more people are willing to work – but the supply curve is a gently sloping one.

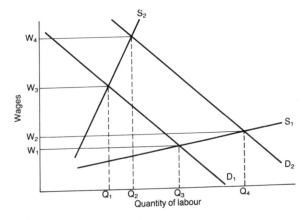

Figure 7 Labour suppy and demand

The level of wages (W_1) is determined by the intersection of this supply curve (S_1) and the demand for labour (D_1), at which point the quantity of labour employed is Q_3.

Suppose that, as a result of an increase in demand for the goods produced by the industry, extra workers are required at all wage rates. The demand for labour moves out to D_2. The effect is a small increase in wages, from W_1 to W_2, and a proportionately larger increase in the number of workers employed, from Q_3 to Q_4.

Now consider the position when the industry is unionized. The existence of the union has two principal effects. The first is to impose restrictions on entry by workers into the industry. In the extreme case, where all workers employed have to belong to the union (the industry **closed shop**), the union has ultimate control of the supply of labour. More generally, unions can insist on **entry restrictions** such as five-year apprenticeships to limit the supply of labour.

The other effect is to give workers as a whole the ultimate veto in wage bargaining. An individual worker can threaten to withdraw his labour, but it is an empty threat; the firm can carry on, other workers can be recruited. But when the union threatens to withdraw all labour at once, then the management has to take notice.

Returning to Figure 7, the effect of the union is to achieve a shift in the supply curve for labour. By exerting control over the number of workers entering the industry, and by bargaining collectively on wages, the union produces a much steeper supply curve (S_2).

In the initial situation, with demand D_1, the union attains a higher wage (W_3) but with a smaller number of workers employed (Q_1). When there is an outward shift in demand to D_2, there is a proportionately larger increase in wages (to W_4) than in employment, which increases from Q_1 to Q_2.

The union mark-up

The above analysis suggests that unions achieve higher wages for their members, albeit at the expense of a lower overall level of employment within an industry. Most economists would accept that the principal role of unions is the achievement of higher wages.

Professor Minford of the University of Liverpool calculated that, over the period 1964–79, the union **mark-up** averaged 74 per cent. In other words, union members enjoyed wages 74 per cent higher on average than non-union members.

This comparison was, however, a very broad-brush one, essentially comparing unionized sectors of the economy with non-unionized sectors. Professor Minford described his comparison as between 'the unionized sector including its satellites and the non-unionized parts; think of mineworkers or firemen relative to cleaning ladies or Liverpool taxi drivers'.

Other estimates, based on jobs that are similar and comparing union and non-union wages, have found that a mark-up exists but a smaller one than suggested by Professor Minford. Work at the Institute for Employment Research at Warwick University found a mark-up which ranged from 1 per cent for skilled manual workers, 3 per cent for clerical workers, 4 per cent for middle managers and 10 per cent for semi-skilled manual workers.

If it is indeed the case that unions push up the wages of their members at the expense of employment, then an attack of union power should not result in higher unemployment. But in practice many unions did not conform to the theoretical model. Powerful unions and weak managements often resulted in a situation where the union could insist on both higher wages and higher employment. The high rates of pay and **overmanning** in the newspaper industry were a case in point.

Unions and employment
Union leaders would not admit that they bargain principally on pay and accept lower employment as a consequence. They would say that the more that trade unionism is spread over the economy, the greater is the dispersion of the twin benefits of high pay and high employment. Worker is not taking from worker, although workers as a whole may be claiming a bigger share of national income at the expense of profits.

The experience of the 1980s has provided a testing ground for the motives of trade unions. During the 1979–81 recession – and subsequently – there were many instances where the unions faced a choice between accepting pay cuts for their members, or large-scale redundancies. In all but a handful of cases the unions accepted redundancies.

This experience tallies with theories of the labour market which suggest that it is far from perfect in its operation. In the so-called **insider–outsider models** of the labour market, there are two distinct components of the labour force. The insiders are those people who are in work, and probably represented by unions, or who are on the fringe of work, having recently been in a job. The outsiders are those who have been unemployed for a long time (for example a steelworker in his fifties made redundant several years ago) or who have never worked (for example the school leaver). These outsiders are not represented in the labour market by the unions, and they are regarded as disadvantaged by employers, because they do not have appropriate skills or because their skills have gone rusty through lack of use.

It follows that the outsiders have very little influence on the labour market – they could as well be in Australia for their influence on Britain's labour market. While a relatively small increase in the demand for labour could quickly absorb all those insiders who are on the fringe of work, and then start pushing up wages, even a very large increase in the demand for labour could leave the outsiders unaffected. This is one reason why the government, along with others around the world, targets its special employment and training measures at the young and the long-term unemployed.

Closed shops

Workers join unions because of the observed fact that union members – or at least those industries and firms that are unionized – apparently receive higher wages. (Apparently, because there are many instances where the opposite seems to be true. The financial services industry, 'the City', is well paid but low on union representation.)

A person working for a firm that is predominantly unionized can, however, gain the wage and other benefits of membership without actually belonging, because employers may not, in practice, discriminate between union and non-union employees. The individual can act as a **free rider**, receiving the benefits, essentially, of other people's union subscriptions. This is one reason why unions like closed shops – agreements with the management that all people employed in the firm should belong to a specified trade union. The other reason, of course, is that a closed shop provides unions with greater clout in negotiations.

Industrial action

The right to strike, for a worker to withdraw his or her labour over a grievance, is regarded as a fundamental one by most trade unionists. Employers often see things differently, regarding a strike as a breach of contract. It has long been the case in English law that the employers' interpretation of a strike as a breach of contract is the correct legal one, but for most of the post-war period until the 1980s few employers invoked the law in this context.

Industrial action can take forms other than strikes over a grievance affecting a particular group of workers. There can be, for example, an impasse in pay negotiations or a deterioration in working conditions, followed by industrial action which does not go as far as a strike – such as an overtime ban or a **work-to-rule**.

There is also industrial action that is not directly related to grievances with the employer. There may be political strikes, or action taken in sympathy with workers in entirely different firms or industries. This **secondary action** may also produce secondary picketing, when workers try to disrupt, not just the factory where the dispute began, but suppliers and customers of that factory.

Trade union reform under Mrs Thatcher

There have been four main pieces of trade union legislation under Mrs Thatcher. The legislation in place is as follows.

The 1980 Employment Act

This Act gave employers the power to take legal action against secondary picketing – attempts to disrupt business away from the picket's own workplace. For example the electricity industry would be able to seek legal remedies against striking miners who tried to stop coal deliveries to power stations.

It also gave employers legal remedies against secondary industrial action – action not directly aimed at the employer involved in the industrial dispute. Again, the electricity industry would be entitled to take legal action against its employees if they had been persuaded by the coal miners not to handle coal at the power stations.

The right of unions to claim trade union recognition from employers was removed. Such recognition could still be claimed but without any statutory backing.

It was made easier for small businesses to dismiss workers without having to go through lengthy unfair dismissal proceedings.

The Act allowed people with conscientious objections to union membership or other strongly held views to opt out of union membership, even in closed shops.

Finally, the Act provided funding for **postal ballots** on industrial action or other matters. The aim was to produce a move away from the 'show of hands' method of deciding on industrial action, where individual union members could be pressured into voting for strikes even if they did not want them. As importantly, the move was seen as bringing about an improvement in trade union democracy, and a shift away from the situation in which militants achieved positions of power in the unions with ease.

The 1982 Employment Act

This Act made it possible for employers to take legal action against trade unions over industrial disruptions. Previously, action was only permitted against individual union organizers in firms.

Employers were given legal remedies against political strikes – those strikes where there is no dispute between employers and their own employees, or where the strike is not over employment matters. For example, employers could seek damages against workers taking part in 'days of action' over the banning of trade unions at the government's Communications Headquarters (GCHQ) at Cheltenham – unless, of course, the employer is the GCHQ itself.

The Act introduced the protection of the law for all employees and for employers against closed shops that have not been approved by an overwhelming majority of the workforce. Further, it made contracts which specified 'union labour only' illegal.

The 1984 Trade Union Act

This legislation required elections to the executive positions within unions (that is senior trade union officials) to be by direct, secret ballot, normally by post.

It gave an additional incentive for the holding of strike ballots by means of secret voting. This would, henceforth, be a condition of the legal immunity of trade unions in organizing industrial action. Employers could sue for damages against strikes called without such a ballot.

The Act required unions to ballot their members every ten years on the continuation of political funds. (The majority of unions operate political funds and donate money to the Labour party.) This was seen as a potential weakening of the link between the trade union movement and Labour. Perhaps as importantly, it threatened Labour's long-term financial position.

Further union reforms

The government made it clear that it did not intend to let its push for union reform rest with the three Acts outlined above. In February 1987 it published a **Green Paper** (a discussion document on which comment is invited) called 'Trade unions and their members'. This contained a number of proposals which followed on from the earlier legislation:

- There was to be a further attempt to discourage closed shops by ending any legal protection for closed shops and making industrial action to enforce them unlawful.
- Members of unions were to be protected from disciplinary action by their unions if they refused to take part in industrial disputes.

- Strike ballots were to be given extra force by allowing union members to prevent unions from calling industrial action without a ballot, and requiring that the ballot must come out with a majority of members in favour before the industrial action goes ahead.
- Ballots for union executives were to be made fully postal and independently supervised and to apply to all union presidents and general secretaries.
- There were to be restrictions on the use of union funds – in particular, preventing funds being used in contravention of court orders. Union members were to be given the right to inspect union accounts.
- A new Commission for Union Affairs was to be set up to fund legal action by individuals or groups of union members against their unions.

The main provisions of the paper became law in May 1988, as the Employment Act 1988.

Union membership statistics

Mrs Thatcher's success in her battle with the trade unions is, on the face of it, perfectly demonstrated by the fact that union membership has shown a marked decline during her time in office.

As Table 6 shows, 1979 was a watershed year for the trade union movement in two respects. Firstly, a government was elected which set out in a determined way to reduce union power. Secondly, Mrs Thatcher's election victory coincided with an all-time high for the number of union members, a level which will probably never again be reached.

Before investigating the subsequent sharp decline in union membership, let us look briefly in a little more detail at the union statistics contained in Table 6. Even at the 1986 figure of 335, which is nearly 140 lower than ten years' earlier, there are a large number of unions in Britain. This has often been cited as a reason for Britain's lack of industrial success compared with countries like West Germany, which has a smaller number of unions and where one union per plant is the norm.

However, there are a large number of very small unions in Britain which are relatively unimportant in the overall picture. In 1986 there were 174 unions – over half the total – with fewer than 1000 members each; and these unions together accounted for only 0.4 per cent (52000) of total union membership. By contrast, there were nine large unions with around 250000 members or more, which together accounted for 55.6 per cent of all union members. At the end of 1986, the top ten unions were: the Transport & General Workers' Union (1 377 944), the Amalgamated Engineering Union (857 559), the General, Municipal, Boilermakers & Allied Trades Union (814 084), the National & Local Government Officers' Association (750 430), the National Union of Public Employees (657 633), the Association of Scientific, Technical & Managerial Staffs (390 000), the Union of Shop, Distributive & Allied Workers (381 984), the Electrical, Electronic, Telecommunication & Plumbing Union (336 155), the Union of Construction, Allied Trades & Technicians (249 485), and TASS (241 000).

Table 6 Figures for trade union numbers and membership

	Number of unions at end of year	Total membership at end of year (000)	Change in membership on previous year (%)
1975	470	12,026	–
1976	473	12,386	+3.0
1977	481	12,846	+3.7
1978	462	13,112	+2.1
1979	453	13,289	+1.3
1980	438	12,947	−2.6
1981	414	12,106	−6.5
1982	408	11,593	−4.2
1983	394	11,236	−3.1
1984	375	10,994	−2.2
1985	370	10,821	−1.6
1986	335	10,539	−2.6

Source: *Employment Gazette,* May 1988

Union membership tends to be most concentrated in manufacturing industry, mining, central and local government, the National Health Service, transport and public education. There is, by comparison, a much smaller proportion of union members in private sector service industries.

Why membership has declined
There are three principal reasons for the decline in union membership under Mrs Thatcher. The first, and most important, is the fall in employment in those industries where union representation has traditionally been strongest. Between June 1979 and December 1985,

employment in manufacturing fell from 7.1 million to 5.25 million, a drop of nearly 2 million, a high proportion of which would have been trade union members.

The second reason has been the failure of the unions to make inroads into those sectors where employment is growing fastest. The unions have been slow to recruit in the service industries such as hamburger chains, or in fast-growing production industries such as electronics. Partly this has to do with the type of jobs on offer in the service industries. Much of the growth of employment in Britain since the employment trough of March 1983 has been for part-time workers, and notably for married women. When jobs are regarded as an opportunity for earning money on the side, there is very little incentive for the people who take them to join unions.

In addition, there has been a strong growth in self-employment, which has been rising by over 100000 a year since the early 1980s. The unions have hardly gained a toehold among self-employed people.

The third factor – and the one which has been the least important so far but which is likely to grow in importance in the future – is the government's reform of the unions. Many people undoubtedly belonged to unions because they had to – because they were working in a closed shop. The attack on the closed shop contained in the government's trade union legislation removes this reason for belonging to a union. And the overall reduction in union power and influence is likely to make more prople think twice about joining or remaining members of unions.

Industrial disputes

One of the central aims of the Conservatives' trade union reforms was to achieve industrial peace. For many years the image of Britain was of a country beset with strikes and other industrial disputes, often over apparently trivial matters such as tea breaks. The strike weapon, it appeared, was used as a matter of course and not merely in the last resort.

A way of measuring the success of the reforms is, therefore, to look at the industrial relations record of Mrs Thatcher's governments compared with earlier periods (see Table 7). On the face of it the most recent figures – with days lost due to industrial disputes the lowest since 1963 – support the view that there has been a marked improvement in the industrial relations climate. But before jumping to this conclusion, we need to look at the figures in a little more detail.

Excluding 1979 – the figures for which were affected by public sector industrial disputes in the infamous 'winter of discontent', as well as a long engineering strike, largely before Mrs Thatcher took office – the record is an improved one, but not spectacularly so. In the 1980–86 period an average of 8.68 million working days were lost a year because of industrial stoppages. This compared with 12.87 million days lost a year on average in the 1970s, a period notable for its industrial disruption. In the 1960s fewer than 5 million working days were lost annually.

The record is even less impressive when two other factors are taken into account. These are the high level of unemployment under Mrs Thatcher and the growth in real wages.

Table 7   Figures for industrial stoppages

	Working days lost (000)	Working days lost per 1000 employees	Workers involved (000)	Number of stoppages
1966	2398	103	544	1951
1967	2787	122	734	2133
1968	4690	207	2258	2390
1969	6846	303	1665	3146
1970	10980	489	1801	3943
1971	13551	613	1178	2263
1972	23909	1081	1734	2530
1973	7197	318	1528	2902
1974	14750	647	1626	2946
1975	6012	265	809	2332
1976	3284	146	668	2034
1977	10142	449	1166	2737
1978	9405	413	1041	2498
1979	29474	1274	4608	2125
1980	11964	521	834	1348
1981	4266	195	1513	1344
1982	5313	249	2103	1538
1983	3754	179	574	1364
1984	27135	1280	1464	1221
1985	6402	298	791	903
1986	1920	89	720	1074

Some small stoppages are excluded from these statistics.
Source: *Employment Gazette*, July 1988

Mrs Thatcher inherited an unemployment level of 1.2 million. By the autumn of 1982 it rose to over 3 million, and subsequently reached 3.5 million. As I write this the level has come down to below 3 million, partly as a result of changes in the basis of the figures. It is still, by historical standards, very high. High unemployment, and the threat of redundancy and closure of firms, would normally be expected to act as a constraint on industrial action.

By the middle of 1987 average earnings measured across the whole economy were around 100 per cent higher than at the beginning of 1980. Prices over the same period increased by 64 per cent. The increase in real wages works out at 22 per cent, supporting the view that the unions did best at looking after those in work, to the detriment of the unemployed.

Most of these real wage increases, as some trade union officials have admitted, were easily won. They resulted, in part, from the fact that the inflation performance of the economy consistently came out better than wage bargainers had expected.

Again, large real wage increases would normally be associated with industrial peace. If workers are getting meaningful pay improvements then there should be less incentive for them to take industrial action.

The government would take issue with the charge that high unemployment has acted as a brake on industrial action. Many of the industrial disputes of recent years have been about redundancies and the slimming down of firms and industries – the 1984–85 miners' strike being the classic example. The backdrop of high unemployment, it can be argued, is likely to make unions fight even harder to preserve jobs in such situations, because if redundancies go through their members will have no other jobs to go to.

The government would also say that real wage rises have been earned through higher productivity (output per person employed). And the process of securing these gains in productivity, through changes in working practices and redundancies, has again involved industrial action.

The miners' strike and the Wapping dispute

Two industrial disputes under Mrs Thatcher have been seen as key developments in the history of the trade union movement. The first was the long miners' strike of 1984–85. At issue was the determination of the National Coal Board (now British Coal) to seek to close uneconomic pits. Two features of the bitter and often violent dispute over this issue stand out. The first was the failure of the National Union of Mineworkers to secure effective support from other trade unions. This may have been because other unions feared legal action under the Conservatives' trade union laws if they supported the miners. The second feature was that these laws, perhaps because the threat was enough, were not used to any great extent.

The defeat of the miners was mainly due to the sharp build-up of coal stocks at the power stations before the strike started. There was also a willingness to spend public money, notably on policing but also on allowing through larger pay settlements for other groups of public sector workers than might otherwise have been the case. The Chancellor of the Exchequer described this additional spending as a good investment.

The second key dispute was between News International and the print unions over a new plant at Wapping in East London. In January 1986, Rupert Murdoch announced his plans to produce a new London evening newspaper, the *London Post*, at Wapping. After failing to secure union representation on terms they could accept, the print unions announced their intention of taking industrial action. When Murdoch said that new contracts would apply throughout his existing titles (*The Sun, News of the World, The Times* and *The Sunday Times*) including a no-strike agreement, the print unions – the National Graphical Association and SOGAT 82 – called their members out on strike.

News International, using pre-Thatcher legislation, immediately dismissed the 5500 workers involved for breach of contract, scrapped plans for the *London Post*, and shifted production of the existing titles to the Wapping plant.

This time, the Conservative union laws were used, notably to prevent secondary industrial action. The print unions were prevented from calling out their members in other newspapers in sympathy, or from stopping their members handling News International titles at wholesalers.

This dispute continued into 1987 and was, at times, as bitter and violent as the miners' strike. But because the workers involved had been dismissed and because production of the newspapers continued, it did not feature in the statistics for days lost because of industrial disputes. Thus, the 1986 figures for industrial stoppages cannot be exactly equated with industrial peace.

The miners' strike and the Wapping dispute have left the unions in a weaker position. It now appears that determined employers, with the backing of the government, can defeat the big guns of the union movement. It is also the case that the two disputes have produced sharp divisions within the trade union movement. The National Union of Mineworkers is in bitter conflict with the breakaway Union of Democratic Mineworkers. The traditional print unions, the NGA and SOGAT 82, are implacably opposed to the Electrical, Electronic,

Telecommunication & Plumbing Union (EEPTU), which they see as having made inroads into printing jobs, notably at Wapping.

Unemployment and productivity

During the run-up to the 1987 general election, much was made of the transformation of the British economy, and of something approaching a British **productivity** miracle. There is a good deal of anecdotal evidence of new attitudes in Britain's factories and, indeed, of better productivity performance.

In the later part of 1987 and early in 1988, productivity in manufacturing industry, measured in terms of output per person employed, was rising at rates of 7 and 8 per cent a year – high by historical standards. The result was that pay increases, with average earnings in manufacturing growing by around 8.5 per cent, could largely be justified in terms of productivity improvements.

However, productivity growth tends to vary according to the position of the economy within the cycle. During strong periods of growth, productivity growth is rapid. When growth is weak, productivity slows. Economists have agreed that there has been an improvement in productivity in the 1980s, but that the underlying rate of productivity growth in manufacturing – at around 4 per cent – has been well below average earnings increases. Thus, unless earnings growth slows markedly as economic growth moderates – which recent experience suggests it will not do – then there are potential problems for the economy in years to come.

It is important to remember when assessing the productivity improvements under Mrs Thatcher (and the frequently quoted evidence that Britain was at the bottom of the major countries' productivity league in the 1960s and 70s and at the top in the 80s) that there are two components to productivity growth. The two components of 'output per person employed' are output and employment. Productivity can increase simply be producing the same output with fewer people. This, in large part, characterizes the productivity gains in manufacturing industry in Britain in the 1980s.

Between 1979 and the middle of 1987, output per person employed in manufacturing in Britain rose by over a third. There was no net increase in manufacturing output over this period – output in the middle of 1987 was virtually the same as its 1979 average, having dipped sharply in the early 1980s.

The productivity improvement came from the fact that over a quarter of manufacturing jobs were lost over the period. In broad terms, in 1987 three workers were producing what it used to take four to do. This is a substantial gain in productivity, but arguably a less desirable one than when output is rising strongly and employment is stable, as appeared to be the case in 1987–88.

Some economists have questioned the extent of genuine productivity gains at the factory level. The 'batting average' view of productivity improvement is that it resulted from the closure of inefficient factories and not necessarily from productivity gains in the remaining ones, in the same way that leaving out the worst players from a cricket team would improve the batting average for those remaining.

For the economy as a whole the productivity gains of the 1980s have been rather less impressive than in manufacturing alone. The growth rate of output per person employed for the whole economy, which averaged around 2 per cent over the 1979–87 period, has been no better than the long-run growth of productivity in Britain.

KEY WORDS	
Corporatism	Industrial action
Closed shop	Work-to-rule
Entry restrictions	Secondary action
Mark-up	Postal ballots
Overmanning	Green Paper
Insider–outsider models	Productivity
Free rider	

Reading list

Davies, Gavyn, *Governments Can Affect Unemployment*, Employment Institute 1985.

Hayek, F.A., *1980s Unemployment and the Unions*, Institute of Economic Affairs, 1980.

Layard, Richard, *How to Beat Unemployment*, Oxford University Press, 1986.

Levačić, R., *Supply Side Economics*, Heinemann Educational Books, 1988.

Meade, J.E., *Wage-Fixing Revisited*, 2nd edn, Institute of Economic Affairs, 1985.

Morris, Derek (ed.), *The Economic System in the UK*, 3rd edn, Oxford University Press, 1985. Chapters 4 and 11 are relevent to this chapter, but the whole book can be recommended.

Essay Topics

1. 'The taming of the unions owes more to high unemployment than to the government's trade union reforms.' Discuss.

2. Does the experience of high unemployment combined with rising real wages since 1979 support the argument that trades unions are effective in wage bargaining but ineffective in preventing large-scale redundancies? Examine with reference to the idea that the labour market consists of 'insiders' and 'outsiders'.
3. Describe the closed shop and secondary industrial action. How has the government's trade union legislation since 1979 restricted the action of trades unions in these areas?
4. Explain the relationship between output, employment and productivity. What are the causes of the growth of productivity in Britain since 1979?
5. 'The unions have lost members in the old industries and failed to recruit in the new industries.' Discuss with reference to patterns of trade union membership since 1979. Are there other reasons for the changes in trade union membership that have occurred?
6. What is the union mark-up? Does the government's anti-closed-shop legislation make it easier for an individual to take advantage of the union mark-up without belonging to a trade union?
7. 'High unemployment and rising real wages have produced industrial peace.' Present the case for and against this statement.
8. Why has the growth in employment since 1983 not been accompanied by a rise in union membership? Why has this growth not produced a sharper fall in unemployment?

Data Response Question 7

Core and periphery

Read the accompanying article from *The Times* of 21 March 1986.

1. Why is pay in Britain 'breaking all the rules'?
2. Would you expect pay settlements to be higher or lower in areas of high unemployment?
3. What is meant by the core and the periphery of the labour market?
4. How does this analysis (the core and periphery) help explain large pay settlements at a time of high unemployment?
5. What other reason could there be for regional similarities in pay? Why is this not thought to offer an explanation in this case?
6. How does the inflexibility of the housing market affect the labour market?
7. What are the two main conclusions about pay settlements?
8. What factors determine pay settlements?

9. What are economists said to favour as the means by which governments could reduce unemployment?
10. Incomes policy is said to be 'out of bounds'. What is being introduced to encourage pay moderation, and how might this work?

High pay settlements defy jobless figures

Pay in Britain appears to be breaking all the rules. It has responded, but not as much as could have been expected, to the sharp rise in unemployment since the late 1970s.

The best hope, as the Chancellor has said, is that it will now respond to the prospect of 3 per cent inflation and the bonus of a cut in the basic rate of income tax.

Why is pay still increasing at a rate that is well above inflation, in spite of high unemployment? Figures published by the Confederation of British Industry, when taken with the official unemployment data, support an argument that is gaining popularity among economists.

It is that the unemployed in general, and the long-term unemployed in particular, have little influence on the pay bargaining process. Pay is determined by what is happening in the core of the employed labour force, and hardly affected by the periphery of the unemployed and some casual and part-time workers on the fringe of the labour market.

The CBI's regional evidence shows that pay settlements are remarkably uniform across the country, in spite of wide variations in regional unemployment rates.

This is not mainly because pay is negotiated nationally. A large proportion of the settlements are for small and medium-sized companies, and locally negotiated.

The CBI's figures show up one or two

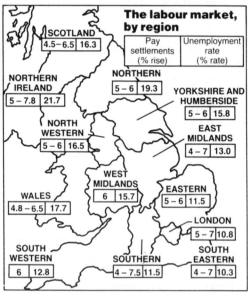

The labour market, by region

	Pay settlements (% rise)	Unemployment rate (% rate)
SCOTLAND	4.5–6.5	16.3
NORTHERN IRELAND	5–7.8	21.7
NORTHERN	5–6	19.3
YORKSHIRE AND HUMBERSIDE	5–6	15.8
NORTH WESTERN	5–6	16.5
EAST MIDLANDS	4–7	13.0
WEST MIDLANDS	6	15.7
WALES	4.8–6.5	17.7
EASTERN	5–6	11.5
LONDON	5–7	10.8
SOUTH WESTERN	6	12.8
SOUTHERN	4–7.5	11.5
SOUTH EASTERN	4–7	10.3

oddities. Whereas the average pay increase across the country is 5 to 6 per cent, in Northern Ireland, with an unemployment rate of nearly 22 per cent – 8 points above the national average – pay settlements are a little higher, at 5 to 7.8 per cent.

The regional reports from the CBI also highlight other things that are happening in the labour market. The Northern region, with unemployment of just under 20 per cent has some skill shortages. These are also reported, particularly among management and financial personnel, in Northern Ireland.

In the North West, with a 16.5 per cent jobless rate, union negotiators are laying stress, not only on inflation, which should be good for prospects of lower settlements, but also on healthy company profitability, which is pulling in the other direction.

As worrying for the Chancellor is the tendency for pay pressure to arise, not from the path of inflation, but from large and well-publicized price increases.

In the CBI's Eastern region, covering East Anglia, big increases in local authority rates – Cambridgeshire is putting rates up by 33 per cent – have been a factor in pay talks, and the regional office concludes that pay settlements are likely to remain significantly above the overall inflation rate.

One popular argument for the apparent failure of the labour market in Britain is that the housing market is rigid and inflexible and so workers are unable to move to where the work is. Thus, they drop out of the core of the market, rather than remaining within it in another area.

The CBI's Southern region, which includes the Thames Valley reports that the housing market is exerting an influence on both employment and pay. Housing is in short supply and expensive, according to the regional report, and is deterring workers from moving to the area, even when jobs are available.

There are two main conclusions. The first is that high levels of unemployment do not appear to exert a moderating influence on pay settlements.

The second is that, even when the rate of inflation drops to 3 per cent in the near future, pay increases will not automatically fall into line.

It is possible to view the labour market as a perfect market, in which the existence of large numbers of unemployed people would automatically push down pay levels.

In this model of the labour market, employers would quickly take on new workers from among the unemployed if pay rises for the existing workforce were too large.

In practice, and for a number of reasons, this does not seem to work.

Pay is determined through a complex interaction of inflation prospects, how well the company is doing, how strong the union's organization is and the extent to which management thinks that a cost increase can be passed on.

This is why the majority of economists have moved away from the idea of a general reflation to reduce the jobless total, to targeting any state employment-reducing measures directly at the long-term unemployed.

This leaves open the question of overall pay increases in the economy. They do not respond fully to higher unemployment or a declining rate of inflation.

Incomes policy remains strictly out of bounds for the present, leaving the proposed expansion of company profit-sharing schemes as the preferred route to pay moderation.

David Smith
Economics Correspondent

Data Response Question 8
Wages and inflation

Read the accompanying article from *The Times* of 1 April 1985.

1. The pound's rise has had an immediate effect on prices. How?
2. Why are the 'inflationary warning signals' flashing?
3. Why might a stronger pound lead to some extra inflation?
4. What is the 'biggest inflation threat'?
5. What do you understand by unit wage costs?
6. How much have these accelerated by since 1983?

7. What does Professor Meade describe as the 'two extremes' of wage-fixing arrangements?
8. What is his middle ground?
9. What three conditions would employers have to fulfil to satisfy wage tribunals?
10. What would trade unions have to give up under Professor Meade's scheme?

Wage fixing revisited – with impeccable timing

The pound, a month ago hobbling towards the knackers' yard, is now up and bounding around like a two-year old. It has been a remarkable recovery, 20 per cent against the dollar and more than 10 per cent on the sterling index in four weeks.

There has been an immediate effect on prices. This weekend petrol prices were reduced to just under £2 a gallon. The gentle downward trawl of base rates from their January crisis levels assuming the pound's buoyancy continues, should produce lower mortgage rates by the summer.

Despite these favourable effects, inflation warning signals are flashing for Britain.

There has been a sharp rise in industry's costs in the 12 months to February: the cost of materials bought by manufacturing industry (other than food, drink and tobacco) rose by 14.9 per cent. Prices charged by companies in this category have been rising strongly. In February there was a 0.8 per cent increase in output prices, to stand 6.5 per cent up on a year earlier. In January the rate was 6.3 per cent, in December 5.7 per cent.

It may be that this is simply a producer price bulge, directly resulting from sterling's earlier sharp drop, and providing a one-off boost inflation but not necessarily a permanent switch to a higher inflation plane.

Another interpretation can be made. This is that the falling pound may have restrained some price rises in Britain, providing an explanation for the muted effect on inflation of sterling's depreciation. The argument is that when the pound is falling companies can take both bigger margins and higher volumes on exports and so do not need to raise domestic selling prices as much as would normally be required.

This effect comes to an end when the pound rises and, while input costs may rise at a slower rate, output prices could rise still faster in the months ahead, with a direct feed through to retail price inflation.

House prices, an important indicator of inflationary pressures in the economy, are rising at a faster rate than they should be, considering record real mortgage rates. Survey evidence suggests a 2–2.5 per cent rise in the first quarter, and a likely 10–15 per cent rise for the year as a whole.

There is also a straight monetary explanation of why the risks on inflation are mostly on the upside. Money supply growth, on the broad sterling M3 measure, was outside the Government's target range for much of the past year, only creeping back inside in the last two months.

Sterling's present strength may reflect the fact that the authorities are overcompensating for earlier monetary laxity, but again there are elements of locking the stable door after inflation has bolted.

Inevitably, though, wage costs stand out as the biggest inflation threat. A feature of the past three years has been the stubborn refusal of the growth of earnings to moderate. This was less important when productivity growth was very strong, it is particularly important now that productivity growth has slowed.

In the fourth quarter of 1983, unit labour costs in manufacturing were rising at a rate of 0.7 per cent a year. Since then the position has deteriorated sharply. By the fourth quarter of last year, unit wage costs were up 5.4 per cent on a year earlier. In January this year, the 12-month rate jumped further, to 6.5 per cent.

The Institute of Economic Affairs has therefore chosen a timely moment to publish Professor James Meade's paper *Wage-Fixing Revisited* (IEA, 2 Lord North St, London SW1, £1.50).

Professor Meade, winner of the Nobel prize for economics in 1977 and one of the authors of the 1944 White Paper on employment policy – the successor to which was published last week – addresses a familiar theme. Wage determination is the central problem facing democratic economies and, without a radical change in the system of wage-fixing in Britain, the alleviation of unemployment will only be achieved at the expense of far higher inflation.

Professor Meade rejects the two "extremes" of a centralized incomes policy and a perfectly competitive labour market, the former because it would imply excessive government interference, the latter because it would require politically unacceptable moves, for example the cutting off of benefits to the unemployed.

The middle ground he suggests, lies in a series of independent wage tribunals. These impartial tribunals, whose decision would be final, would, in the Meade scheme decide in favour of employees' pay claims unless the employers could show that their offer satisfied three conditions.

These are first, that output would be appreciably higher in the long run if the offer, rather than the workers' claim, was instituted. Second, that the offer was within a reasonable range of an overall wage guideline, of say 5 per cent, for the economy. Finally, that the offer did not push the relative pay of the employees more than perhaps 3 per cent below its average over the previous five years.

In other words, companies would have to demonstrate to the tribunal that their offer was good for employment in the long-term but did not impose an excessive squeeze on the relative wages of its workers.

In return for the introduction of wage tribunals, trade unions would be required to give up all the legal privileges and immunities conferred upon them in the 1906 Trade Disputes Act, Professor Meade says. Additional penalties against industrial action, including treating the beginning of a strike as the end of a period of employment for redundancy purposes, and only paying benefits to strikers' families on condition that they would be repaid after the strike, are also included in the scheme.

This mixture of the tough and tender smacks of the SDP/Liberal Alliance approach to wage control, hardly surprising in view of the fact that Professor Meade has been prominent in the formulation of Alliance economic policy.

Professor Meade's paper also endorses the inflation tax proposal of Professor Richard Layard, under which companies would suffer a tax penalty if they increased wages above a generally agreed ceiling.

The interesting question is the extent to which Nigel Lawson, in his Budget a fortnight ago, was stealing the Alliance's clothes. The Budget changes in national insurance contain elements of a Layard-type inflation tax.

The removal of the upper earnings limit on employers' contributions imposes a clear penalty upon large pay increases for already well-paid workers. At the lower end, the new graduated scale of National Insurance contributions, for both employers and employees, also discourages big percentage pay rises.

However, if the Lawson national insurance changes are to be regarded as an inflation tax, they are clearly a modest one. More radical action to control pay is still needed.

David Smith
Economics Correspondent

Chapter Six
Conclusions

Mrs Thatcher's period in office, now in its third Parliamentary term, has provided a rich vein of material for those wishing to examine economic policy in practice. Many of the policy changes introduced in 1979 represented abrupt changes in direction; and, perhaps more than with any other post-war government, the aims were set out at the start and can easily be compared with the actual results.

We can conclude by reminding ourselves of the themes of Mrs Thatcher's economic policy in practice, as they have been brought out in this book. The first theme is the gradual shift away from rigid ideas about economic management and a steady shift towards pragmatism.

Thus, as we saw in Chapter 2, strict monetary targets proved to be more of a problem than an aid for policy-makers. Blindly following targets was not something which offered much assistance in the real world. The move has been back to the old ways of gearing monetary policy mainly towards securing a particular level for the exchange rate.

This theme also carries us on to the government's record on public expenditure control, which we examined in Chapter 3. Ambitious plans to secure large real cuts in public spending gave way to realism. The target moved to that of holding spending constant and, finally, to allowing it to increase, but at a slower rate than the rest of the economy.

Again, very clearly, we have seen a move away from rigid policy ideas towards pragmatism and realism.

The second broad theme we can detect is that the government appears to have achieved more success in fulfilling its aims with microeconomic policy than with macroeconomic policy. The broad macroeconomic policies of monetary control and reining back public spending have been compromised.

On the other hand, within the broad aim of reining back the public sector, the microeconomic policy of privatization has, in its own terms, been a notable success. This is not to say that privatization has satisfied everyone – the post-privatization performance of British Telecom has been the cause of loud complaint. But in the narrow sense of transferring state industries to the private sector, privatization has been more successful than the Conservatives could have hoped. The same is true for council house sales.

This theme carries us through to Chapter 4 and tax cuts. There has been no overall reduction in the tax burden. For most people, tax paid as a proportion of income was higher after eight years of Conservative control. But if we take the narrow aim of reducing income tax alone, there has been a measure of success.

The government's trade union reforms, as we saw in Chapter 5, are also a microeconomic or supply-side policy. Here, as with privatization, the achievement in shifting the balance of power back to employers from the unions has gone beyond Conservative hopes. Whether it could have come about without high unemployment is a matter of some debate.

Through a combination of accident and design, Mrs Thatcher has changed Britain's economic landscape, to the point where the clock can never be turned back to the old model of the 1960s and 70s. The interesting question is to what extent future governments – be they Conservative, Labour, or Social and Liberal Democratic – will seek to take the economy in a different direction.

Index